THE
GOLDEN AGE
OF THE
COUNTRY
HOUSE

Christopher Simon Sykes

Foreword by Nigel Nicolson

MAYFLOWER BOOKS · NEW YORK CITY

To Christopher IV

AUTHOR'S NOTE

Almost all the photographs in this book have been taken
from private family albums, and I have relied wherever
possible on their original captions in identifying the people,
places and dates. In the absence of such information, I have
made every effort to supply accurate details from other
sources, but should like to apologise for any mistakes which
may have occurred as a result.

C.S.S.

Library of Congress Cataloging in Publication Data
Sykes, Christopher Simon, 1948–
The golden age of the country house.
London ed. published under title: Country house camera.
1. England – Social life and customs – 19th century – Pictorial works.
2. England – Social life and customs – 20th century – Pictorial works.
3. Country life – England – Pictorial works. 4. Country homes – England –
Pictorial works. 5. Photography – England – History. I. Title.
DA533.S985   1980   779'.9'94208   79-23490
ISBN 0-8317-3945-2

MANUFACTURED IN GREAT BRITAIN
FIRST AMERICAN EDITION

CONTENTS

Foreword

The techniques and art of photography developed remarkably soon after it was invented. Only twenty years separate Fox Talbot's famous photograph of the latticed window at Lacock Abbey from amateur snapshots which were as good as most of us can manage today. The nineteenth century suddenly came alive. Before the invention, there were professional portraits, invariably flattering, of aristocrats dressed in finery and posed against contrived backgrounds of equivalent dignity, and they were painted slowly, allowing every opportunity to alter them to suit the artist's taste or the sitter's vanity. Only rarely were more than two or three figures shown – a family conversation-piece with dogs and horses, but seldom friends.

Then people began to photograph each other, standing or reclining casually in day-clothes, sometimes whole groups of them, and there is a gawky untidiness about the earliest pictures in this book which painted portraits had carefully avoided. People at first appear stiffer than they actually were, their clothes dowdier, their expressions less mobile, and of course there was no colour. The subjects were required to remain still for several minutes; they stare at the camera or at each other with grim concentration. It was not inappropriate to the mid-century that the camera first caught people at their sternest and most austere. Even the children seem cowed, and the houses lack lustre. The sun seldom seems to shine.

But here at last are people with whom we feel we could communicate. Throughout history, men and women have been sprawling, grimacing, belching and dying, but now the camera catches them at it. For the first time we see them off-guard, sometimes from behind, often in mid-gesture. Contemporaries began to see themselves as others saw them, and the experience must have been as strange as it still is for us when first we hear our recorded voices. People began to exclaim, as they have never ceased exclaiming, 'It's lovely of you, but terrible of me.' It must

have been difficult to persuade the old or the plain to pose.

It was a magical new game which few could play at a period when the apparatus was cumbersome and expensive, and space for dark-rooms and leisure for experiment were both essential. It is not surprising that amateur photography should first have been regularly practised in the larger country houses. Their successful prints were pasted in leather-bound albums, sometimes fully captioned and dated, but more often left to speak for themselves until the identities of those photographed faded from family memory.

Mr Sykes has given us an entrancing selection from the thousands that survive. Familiar as many of their surnames are, his amateurs, the majority of them the ladies or daughters of the house, never sought or found fame for their photographs. They practised their small domestic art for fun, as they might play the piano, or diabolo. Members of the family and staff, and chance visitors, were their victims. The set-piece photograph of a weekend party became a visual visitor's book. They seldom photographed anything but people, but it is people whom we most wish to see, and from these pictures we can assess the whole pattern of social relationships – the dominant patriarch, with his chivalry towards women, the coy children, the proud gamekeeper, the retiring governess, the hierarchy of the kitchen. But also evident are affection, linking the generations, sexes and classes, and a confidence that life would go on unchanged.

As in fact it did. The permanence of Victorian attitudes is the main impression made by the first fifty of these years. Then, when the Queen died and the century with her, we begin to sense something new. The faces of the young men fated to die in Flanders have a contemporary look. With faster film, the camera discovered the laugh, the comic smirk, the theatrical pose, and an old man learning to ride a bicycle. The motor-car appeared (leading, as Mr Sykes says with perhaps unconscious wit, 'to a faster turn-over of guests'), and we find ourselves after the First War in the period of bright young things who took over country houses like Wilton and Plas Newydd from newly indulgent parents. The houses themselves look lovelier, the people more relaxed, with a quality of dash and humour which the drooping moustaches of the previous generation had denied them.

This book, by preserving irreplaceable documents that might soon be lost, illustrates nearly one hundred years of the British upper-class life-style to supplement the written record. From the very beginning the photographs are often beautiful, sometimes funny, invariably tender. Mr Sykes's enjoyment in collecting and selecting them is as evident as that of the photographers who thus immortalized, by the click of a shutter, their families and friends.

NIGEL NICOLSON

INTRODUCTION

THERE IS NOTHING, neither words nor the most detailed or atmospheric painting, that can evoke the past so powerfully and so completely as a photograph. What we see when we look at one is not the possible figment of an artist's imagination, but a scene recorded by the camera just as it was, a shadow in time frozen on glass. Unconsciously we are convinced that, had we too stood alongside the family group on the steps, swung the croquet mallet on the sweeping lawns, or ridden in the carriage, we should have experienced these things exactly as they appear in the photograph. It is this fundamental belief in their authenticity which explains the melancholy that is so often attached to photographs of people no longer living, or buildings which have disappeared. Few documents can convey this sense of nostalgia more profoundly than a country house photograph album.

One of the reasons for this is that the golden age of photography coincided with that of the country house. In the seventeenth and eighteenth centuries the country house was regarded first and foremost as a seat of power, a symbol of the immense wealth and importance of its owner. As a home it had less significance. The family of a gentleman spent most of their time at their town house, visiting the country for as little as three or four months in the year. It was not just that travel was slow and difficult. In the town they met their friends from other parts of the country, while the daughters of the family had the chance to meet young men; they arranged their business, and learned of all the latest developments in politics, the sciences and the arts that had taken place since their previous visit. It was with the accession of Queen Victoria that this pattern began to change, and two influences more than any other helped bring this about: a new emphasis on family life led to a greater enjoyment of the quieter pleasures of the country home, while the advent of the railways made it far more accessible. Suddenly the country house found itself coming to life for up to nine months of the year rather than four.

In many ways the English country house can claim to have been the birthplace of photography. The earliest photographic negative in existence, made in August 1835, is of the diamond-latticed windows of Lacock Abbey, a beautiful Gothic house in Wiltshire. This was the home of William Henry Fox Talbot, grandson of the 2nd Earl of Ilchester and Whig Member of Parliament for Chippenham, to whom must be given much of the credit for the invention of photography as we know it today. Educated at Harrow and Trinity College, Cambridge, he was a gentleman of science, a mathematician and a keen botanist, but first and foremost he was an inventor. It was while on the Grand Tour of Europe in August 1833 with Constance, his bride of a few months, that Fox Talbot became obsessed with the idea of fixing the images cast by a camera obscura with which he was attempting to sketch some Italian landscapes. 'This led me to reflect', he wrote later, 'on the inimitable beauty of the pictures of Nature's painting which the glass lens of the Camera throws upon the paper in its focus – fairy pictures, creations of a moment, and destined as rapidly to fade away. It was

Miss May Rose inserts a dark slide into an early folding hand camera. With its rising front, reflex viewfinder and wide range of shutter speeds, this is the equivalent of one of today's more expensive compact cameras. She is photographed on the lawn of her family's home at Bourton-on-the-Water, Gloucestershire.

during these thoughts that the idea occurred to me how charming it would be if it were possible to cause these natural images to imprint themselves durably, and remain fixed upon the paper. "And why should it not be possible?" I asked myself.'

As soon as he returned to England in 1834, Fox Talbot began experiments using paper sensitized with silver chloride, and within a year he had made his first photograph. This picture of the windows of Lacock Abbey was taken with a tiny two-and-a-half-inch square camera made by a local carpenter. It was christened 'the mousetrap' by Constance, and used a chemically-treated writing paper. The pictures it created were no bigger than an inch square. Lacock Abbey thus became, in Fox Talbot's own words, 'the first building that was ever known to have drawn its own picture'.

The significant feature of his 'pictures' was that they were what are now called negatives. Fox Talbot's most important contribution to the development of what he referred to as 'photogenic drawing' was to start making more than one positive from a negative by placing the negative on top of a second sheet of sensitized paper and exposing this to light through it. This process not only reversed the tones but enabled Fox Talbot to produce an unlimited number of copies from one prototype. His close friend Sir John Herschel, who was himself a pioneer in the field, proposed the name 'negative' for the prototype and 'positive' for the copy. It is on this negative–positive technique that all modern photography depends.

The glory for the invention of photography did not, however, go to Fox Talbot but to a rival of his who, unknown to him, had been working simultaneously in France on his own process. It was Louis-Jacques-Mandé Daguerre, by trade a theatrical designer and creator of grand illusions, who was responsible for turning photography into a craze that swept Europe. Since 1829 he had been working on the experiments of his partner, Joseph-Nicéphore Niépce, who, in 1827, had produced the world's first photographic image. Niépce had named his invention heliography, literally 'sun drawing'. By May 1837 Daguerre had modified this process to such a degree that the exposure time required to produce an image was reduced from eight hours to between twenty and thirty minutes. Moreover, he had also discovered a way of fixing the picture using a solution of common salt. 'I have seized the light! I have arrested its flight!' was his cry of triumph. He named the process daguerreotypy.

To the contemporaries of Daguerre, the very idea that nature could be made to produce a picture spontaneously was quite magical, and the amazement and excitement caused by his revelations were universal. When the news of the publication of Daguerre's results reached Fox Talbot, however, he was bitterly disappointed, frustrated in his hopes 'of being', as he later wrote, 'the first to announce to the world the existence of the New Art, which since has been named Photography'. But, true scientist that he was, he quickly set about improving his

own process, and soon had cut down his exposure times to rival those of the improved daguerreotype. In 1841 he patented his new process as 'calotypy', and in 1844 published an album of actual prints entitled *The Pencil of Nature*. This is the first publication illustrated with photographs. 'The plates of the present work', read the preface, 'are impressed by the agency of light alone without any aid whatsoever from the artist's pencil.'

The public's attitude towards Fox Talbot's work, however, was one of indifference: they preferred the much sharper image of the daguerreotype. But Fox Talbot found an unexpected ally in his own mother, Lady Elizabeth Fielding, who seemed determined to show that, even if the public were not yet ready for her son's invention, then the aristocracy would be. The person she chose to approach was William George Spencer, 6th Duke of Devonshire, a man noted for his interest in the arts, and owner of one of the finest libraries in England. 'My Dear Duke,' she wrote in her first letter to him in the summer of 1846, 'I remember you kindly subscribed to the Sun Pictures in Scotland published by my son last year by way of making known his Discovery of the Photogenic Art as contradistinguished from the Daguerreotype – but probably you never looked at them and as they were sent into the world without any explanation, I hope you will be so amiable as to read one I send you and to accept a few Talbotypes accompanying this, just to show what may be done by this invention.' She went on to suggest that 'in future times I suppose it will be still more perfection'.

Further correspondence followed, and her final letter contains evidence that they met and discussed the subject: 'We are off tomorrow so this is positively my last time of boring you – but I cannot go without leaving you a little specimen of portraits not so *dreadful* as the one that so horrified you last night of the Bard of Erin. The figure spreading paint on his palette is a Finnish painter and very like him and the figure behind is an old Finnish man and his very image.' She concluded: 'The domestic scene in the Cloisters at Lacock Abbey might have been more artistically grouped but it shows what pretty tableaux one may have if people would only *sit still three seconds*, but as they did not it's rather less clear than the others.'

Although Lady Elizabeth's reference to the exposure times is somewhat misleading, as they are likely to have been much longer, by 1846 Fox Talbot had greatly improved his process since the days, not long gone, when exposures of twenty to thirty minutes were often required: days when, in the words of a contemporary photographer, 'the sitters, without wincing, stared fixedly into the direction of that mysterious machine. Coming back again after a time, one would find the same person still sitting in the same position, pinned down to the chair, motionless, speechless, as if asleep with open eyes. . . . And the same with the photographer, always on the same spot, by the mysterious apparatus, a watch in his hand. . . . Everybody was able to understand that there was a secret relation between the young man, the box with the short, cannon-

A scene in the cloisters at Lacock Abbey by Fox Talbot.

like brass tube and the sitter.'

The Duke of Devonshire kept all the prints sent to him by Fox Talbot's mother and stuck them in an album which, still to be found in the library at Chatsworth, is probably one of the earliest of its kind. Although he did not choose to practise photography himself, others of his class did. That English aristocrats should have been amongst the pioneers of the art is less surprising when it is considered how beautifully this new process combined their then fashionable interests. In an age when no lady worth her salt could fail to exhibit some degree of skill with the paint brush or pencil, and when it was not unusual for a gentleman to dabble in the sciences, here was a fascinating new pastime. Moreover, the pursuit of photography, a process bristling with difficulties, had various requirements of which the upper classes, more

than most, were not short: namely time, money and space.

As far as space was concerned, Fox Talbot foresaw this particular problem when he wrote that portrait photography 'must necessarily be in comparatively few hands, because it requires a house to be built or altered on purpose, having an appartment lighted by a skylight etc., otherwise the portrait cannot be taken indoors, generally speaking, without great difficulty.' The attics of a country house would have provided just such a studio, while there was usually any amount of space for a darkroom. Lord Londonderry has recently discovered a Victorian darkroom at Wynyard, the family seat in Northumberland, 'halfway down a rickety old staircase which leads from the old guest wing to the statue gallery on the ground floor'.

In its early days, photography, like most new inventions, was also expensive. In 1850, Horne and

Above *An early group photograph: the coming of age of Lord Lewisham (standing, fifth from left), Patshull House, 1844.*

Opposite *A famous gentleman astronomer, the Earl of Rosse, and his telescope, 1902.*

Thornethwaite, Opticians and Philosophical Instrument Makers, one of the best-known firms dealing in photographic equipment, were offering for sale three different photographic outfits. The price of each of these included a camera and all the required chemicals, as well as knapsack and travelling case. The cost of the outfit varied according to the sizes of the glass plates. That employing five-inch by four-inch plates was £21, six-inch by five-inch £26, while the eight-inch by six-inch outfit was £36. None of these outfits included a portable dark tent, indispensable for anyone wishing to travel with a camera, which cost between £3 and £6 extra. Bringing these prices up to date, this means that anyone wishing to take up photography needed to make a minimum outlay of the equivalent of at least £600, or $1200.

Cuthbert Bede, in a delightful contemporary book, *Photographic Pleasures*, published in 1855, gave an amusing commentary on this aspect of the science:

It is very well for my Lord, or the Squire, who are occasionally ennuied for the lack of amusement, to seek, in calotyping, relief from their magisterial, landlordial and other duties. It is all very well for people who think the purchase of 'a mahogany folding camera, of best construction, with double combination Achromatic lens, mounted in brass front, with rackwork adjustment, sliding front, suitable for views ten inches by eight inches, and portraits eight-and-a-half inches by six-and-a-half inches' – it is all very well for persons who think the purchase of such a piece of furniture as this, a mere fleabite; and can give their twenty-one guineas for it, with no more trouble to themselves, than the trouble it costs them to fill up the cheque. . . . But the cost is widely different when applied to such people as Tom Styles, the ingenious mechanic, or Mr Bibers the chemical-minded hatter, or poor old Pounce the attorney's clerk – all of whom, most probably, have to support wives and numerous pledges of affection, and cannot afford to gratify the best of their inclinations either by the first expenditure in apparatus, or in the continual expense incurred by experimentalising.

Above *Joseph Paxton, the designer of the Crystal Palace, which housed the Great Exhibition.*

Opposite, top left *Augusta Caroline Crofton and her sliding-box camera;* top right *Mary Bulteel and her camera;* bottom left *the Hon. Luke Gerald Dillon and his camera;* bottom right *H. Capper and his camera.*

When thinking of the great early amateur pioneers of photography, the name of Julia Margaret Cameron springs most readily to mind. However, she did not possess a camera until 1863, when given one as a present by her daughter, while there were many unknown country house photographers who had already been hard at work in their darkrooms for several years.

One of these, Lady Lucy Bridgeman, was a daughter of the 2nd Earl of Bradford, and in the early 1850s she took many successful photographs of her family and friends. Most of her work was done at Weston Park, the Bradford family seat in Shropshire, and at the dower house, Castle Bromwich, but she also travelled extensively with her camera to other great houses such as Powis Castle, Scotney Castle and Haddon Hall. She gave great charm and elegance to the groups and family studies, while her portraits possess a natural quality and a clarity which are remarkable for the period in which they were taken. Outstanding among these is the delightful study of her brother and sister-in-law, Lord and Lady Newport, taken at Castle Bromwich (see page 32).

The quality of Lucy Bridgeman's photographs shows just how well she had mastered the tricky problems of early wet-plate photography, a development of Fox Talbot's process by Frederick Scott Archer which had been introduced to the public at the Great Exhibition in 1851. It was a cumbersome and difficult business, involving the use of various highly poisonous chemicals. Collodion containing potassium iodide was first poured on to a glass plate which was carefully tilted until evenly coated. This plate was then sensitized by being immediately dipped into a bath of silver nitrate solution where it remained in darkness for three to five minutes. It then had to be exposed while still moist, because the sensitivity deteriorated rapidly as the collodion dried. Development had to follow directly after exposure, with either pyrogallic acid or ferrous sulphate. The picture was fixed with hyposulphate of soda or potassium cyanide. As the recommended time between the flowing of the collodion and the final development was between eight and ten minutes, the whole process involved a considerable amount of rushing about. Small wonder that one of Julia Margaret Cameron's nieces remembered her 'stained with chemicals from her photography and smelling of them too'.

Above *Lady Jocelyn.*

Opposite *Lady Lucy and Lady Charlotte Bridgeman,*
'The Burnt Aunts', at Castle Bromwich.

Had Lucy Bridgeman lived long enough, she might well have become as celebrated as Julia Margaret. But in the winter of 1858, while still in her early twenties, as she was sitting reading in the library at Weston Park with her sister Charlotte before a blazing log fire, a red-hot ember suddenly landed upon her crinoline. Within a matter of seconds she was, like Miss Haversham, 'running . . . shrieking, with a whirl of fire blazing all about her, and soaring at least as many feet above her head as she was high'. In a desperate attempt to save her sister, Charlotte suffered the same fate. Ever since that night, Lady Lucy and Lady Charlotte Bridgeman have been known in the family as 'The Burnt Aunts'.

Another equally skilful photographer of the same era was Lady Jocelyn. Frances Elizabeth Jocelyn, known as Fanny, was a daughter of Lady Cowper who became the wife of Lord Palmerston. Like Lucy Bridgeman, she was quite unknown outside her own circle, and appears to have been a photographer of considerable talent. She too concentrated on her family and friends, and her studies of herself and her children certainly bear comparison with the better-known work of Viscountess Hawarden who won gold medals in the 1860s for her romantic conversation-pieces on terraces and balconies, and her portraits of children. Fanny Jocelyn also photographed striking house-party groups of Palmerston and his political friends at Broadlands, his family home, and her interiors, such as that shown on pages 38–9, show unusual skill, taken as they were at a time when electric lighting was still unknown.

The type of camera which would have been used by both Lucy Bridgeman and Fanny Jocelyn was almost certainly a sliding-box camera, as this was by far the most popular camera between 1840 and 1865. It consisted of two open-ended boxes, one with a lens fitted to it, the other with the ground-glass or dark-slide. The two boxes slid one within the other for focusing. Later the sliding-box form was replaced by the folding bellows camera.

While Lucy Bridgeman and Fanny Jocelyn were pursuing their new pastime in England, across the water in Ireland Augusta Caroline Crofton, wife of Luke Gerald Dillon, 4th Baron Clonbrock, was also discovering the joys of the new art. She had been introduced to photography by her father, Edward, Baron Crofton of Mote Park, Roscommon, who had bought a camera for her at the Great Exhibition in 1851, and made a 'Photograph House' in the grounds of Mote Park. When she married Lord Clonbrock, he constructed a similar building for her at Clonbrock. It was built in the rustic style, and one can get a good idea of what it must have been like inside from an imaginary description of such a building given by Cuthbert Bede:

The true aristocratic amateur, who can afford both time and money, delights in having a Photographic room fitted up for his own delectation. . . . To the windows he will have an ingenious system of shutters, so as to enable him to exclude daylight, or admit it, at a moment's notice. . . . He will have lamps almost as wonderful as Aladdin's; glass spirit lamps, brass spirit lamps, camphor lamps, argand lamps, lanterns with yellow glass shades, gas jets with metal chimney and gauze. . . . He will have ornamental jars, which will turn out to be filters and holders of

Above *Viscount Dunlo photographs 'Mimi, Alice and Gregory' with his stereoscopic camera at Clonbrock.*

Opposite top *Two unidentified ladies outside the 'Photograph House' at Clonbrock.* Opposite bottom *Theresa Augusta Tighe and Charles St George Crofton, her fiancé, photographed by Augusta Caroline Crofton.*

distilled water. He will have bowls and pans of white china, and dishes of porcelain. . . . His chemical solutions will be arranged on shelves. . . . His fixing solutions and his developing solutions for negatives and positives will all be in lipped bottles. He will have zinc trays, and washing pans, and all the latest fashions in baths. . . . Close at hand he will have quires of bibulous paper, and all the luxuries of his art; – soft camel's-hair brushes, glass filtering funnels, ribbed inside, glass syringes to take up definite quantities of solutions, glass dippers, German beaker glasses and plenty of brass pins. To the shelves around will be pinned sheets of paper for drying; and there will be dark drawers to receive them when they are iodised and made sensitive. . . . Within his reach and hung upon their separate hooks will be an abundant supply of clean linen rags, and pieces of wash leather; and there will be a towelhorse laden with a snowy burden of cloths.

Among the friends who gathered round the Photograph House at Clonbrock were Viscount and Viscountess Dunlo. Viscount Dunlo was the owner of a binocular stereoscopic camera developed from the invention of Sir David Brewster in 1849, and also first introduced at the Great Exhibition. Owing to the small size of each picture, about three by three-and-a quarter inches, and the short five-inch focal length of the lens, it was possible with stereoscopic cameras to obtain instantaneous pictures of moving objects in a fraction of a second. The finished product, two pictures together representing a scene from slightly different angles, was then viewed through a special apparatus called a stereoscope. The extreme popularity in the 1850s of these stereoscopic pictures, usually of foreign views or famous people, not only made a great contribution to bringing photography into the home, but also opened up a new world to the Victorians. 'We have crossed the Andes,' wrote a contemporary columnist, 'ascended Tenerife, entered Japan, "done" Niagara and the Thousand Isles, drunk delight of battle with our peers (at shop windows), sat at the councils of the mighty, grown familiar with kings, emperors and queens, prima donnas, pets of the ballet and "well-graced actors". Ghosts have we seen and have not trembled; stood before royalty and have not uncovered; and looked, in short, through a three-inch lens at every single pomp and vanity of this wicked but beautiful world.'

It is evident, from the fact that their photographs turn up time and time again in each other's albums, that our aristocratic amateurs did not confine themselves solely to their own homes, but moved from house to house with

'Castlewellan Castle Across the Lake': a photograph of his family's home in county Down by the Hon. Hugh Annesley, the second son of William Richard, 3rd Earl Annesley, and Isabella, daughter of the 2nd Earl of Howth. Hugh later became the 5th Earl Annesley. Note the portable dark tent in the bottom left-hand corner.

their cameras. For this purpose many would certainly have had a travelling chest, probably of oak, with their initials and crest engraved upon the lid, and a brass plaque bearing the legend 'GLASS – WITH CARE – THIS SIDE UPPERMOST'. Inside, designed with superb economy of space by the estate carpenter, would lie their bottles of chemicals in little nests and their glass plates in special compartments. In addition to this, they would have carried with them a portable dark tent such as is seen in the photograph, 'Castlewellan Castle Across the Lake', by the Hon. Hugh Annesley.

Some enthusiasts went even further. Lord Kylemore, another Irish peer, had his own 'photographic cab', which was in fact a rather grand carriage converted into a travelling darkroom. This is an idea he may well have adopted from Roger Fenton, who had similarly converted

a wine-merchant's cab to take with him to the Crimea. Roger Fenton, most famous for his photographs of the Crimean War, was himself from the landed classes, the son of John Fenton of Crimble Hall in Lancashire, and much of his finest work was carried out in the country houses of England. Amongst the best are studies of Hardwick Hall, Harewood House, and many of the Royal Family at Windsor Castle.

The reason why the work of Lady Lucy Bridgeman, Lady Jocelyn, Lady Clonbrock, the Hon. Hugh Annesley, and undoubtedly many other as yet unknown country house photographers has remained undiscovered for so long is simple. They practised photography purely for their own amusement and that of their immediate circle. Unlike their famous contemporary, Viscountess Hawarden, who exhibited at the Royal Photographic Society, the results of their work were simply pasted into magnificent albums which were then passed around the family. For example, a cousin of Lady Lucy Bridgeman, the Reverend W. Bridgeman, married Lady Frances Wentworth Fitzwilliam, the daughter of the 5th Earl Fitzwilliam, as a result of which the present Earl Fitzwilliam is the owner of an album which is full of Lady Lucy's photographs. It was probably given to Lucy's cousin as a wedding present. Often these albums were painstakingly and beautifully decorated, doubtless during long winter evenings. This was the perfect opportunity for young ladies to practise their skill in the use of water-colours by creating borders for the pages, frames for the photographs, landscapes or rooms in which to place cut-out figures, and settings for what were often highly elaborate collages. Invariably the eventual fate of most of these albums was to gather dust in an attic; it is only with the recent revival of interest in old photographs, and the subsequent high prices fetched by many albums in the sale rooms, that most of this work has come to light.

Though the work of photographers like Julia Margaret Cameron and Viscountess Hawarden presents us with images of great beauty, painterly in their conception, their photographs are often less of a social document than many found in these great country house albums. For example, the photographs of 'The Dear Servants at Petworth' (see pages 58–60) may individually seem rather dull and unimaginative, hardly in the Julia Margaret class, but as a collection they present us with a fascinating and unique record of an important part of the life of a great house of the period. This series of simple portraits by an unknown photographer was to be echoed many years later in the work of Irving Penn. Similarly Lucy Bridgeman's photographs, which combine both beauty of image and social documentation, and those of the many other unknown photographers in this book, gathered together as they have been from family albums in houses all over Great Britain and Ireland, give a marvellous insight into the different aspects of country house life between the 1850s and the 1930s.

One such aspect is the house-party, in which the owner of a house entertained large numbers of people not related to him. Its origins go back to the middle of the eighteenth century when, during the parliamentary recesses of the 1720s and 1730s, Sir Robert Walpole regularly entertained mixed parties, consisting of his colleagues in the government and a sprinkling of the local gentry, at Houghton, his great house in Norfolk. Here, at these 'congresses', as they were known, the party combined the discussion of politics with eating and drinking on a vast scale, living, in the words of one guest, Lord Hervey, 'up to the chin in beef, venison, geese, turkeys, etc., and generally over the chin in claret, strong beer and punch'. To begin with, these were all-male gatherings, but gradually, as the eighteenth century progressed, and the improvements in roads and transport made the house-party a relatively common event through-out the country, women were included. Soon the country house came to be considered the ideal venue for match-making.

A contemporary description of a house-party at Carton, the Duke of Leinster's house in Ireland, given in 1779, gives a very good idea of the life of such a gathering:

The house was crowded – a thousand comers and goers. We breakfast between ten and eleven, though it is called half-past nine. We have an immense table – chocolate – honey – hot bread – cold bread – brown bread – white bread – green bread – and all coloured breads and cakes. After breakfast Mr Scott, the Duke's chaplain, reads a few short prayers, and we then go as we like – a back room for reading, a billiard room, a print room, a drawing room and whole suites of rooms, not forgetting the music room. . . . There are all sorts of amusements: the gentlemen are out hunting and shooting all the morning. We dine at half-past four or five – go to tea, so to cards about nine . . . play till supper time – 'tis pretty late by the time we go to bed.

As the eighteenth century moved into the nineteenth, society was expanding and, as it did so, the numbers of people to be entertained in the country swelled accordingly. At the same time it became increasingly necessary to find new kinds of entertainment to keep the guests amused. In 1833 the 6th Duke of Devonshire installed a private theatre at Chatsworth as an added recreation for his guests. Soon amateur theatricals became one of the most popular of country house entertainments, usually performed on a temporary stage in a hall or gallery. Billiards became increasingly fashionable, and tables appeared in most houses, often in a special room of their own, an extension perhaps of a bigger room. There were balls and breakfast parties, and every kind of sport.

In the innumerable group photographs that became so fashionable, the country house album provides a perfect record of the house-party in all its various forms. We see Lord Palmerston entertaining his political friends at Broadlands, while at Wilton Lord Pembroke holds a cricket week. At Witley Court, Lord Dudley's guests pose round the great fountain on a summer's day with their model sailing boats. A shooting party, its game at its feet, is grouped on the steps of Warter Priory. At Port Lympne, at the end of the First World War, Sir Philip Sassoon and his sister, Lady Rocksavage, the mistress of Houghton where it all began, entertain the British government and foreign politicians attending the peace conference. Here the wheel has turned almost full circle, as these were amongst the last of the great political house-parties.

Photographs, precisely because of the profound sense of nostalgia which they evoke, have the ability to chronicle change better than any other medium, and it is a story of change that these country house photographs tell when we look at them as a whole. We see how the architecture altered as the results of the Industrial Revolution took effect. As huge new fortunes were made in the towns, and existing ones in the country were swollen by the discovery of coal under the fields, or the spreading of a town over the property, many country house owners

'Ghosts at the Hyde', an ingenious experiment by an amateur made in the 1890s.

competed with one another to increase the splendour of their residences, often in order to match the new ones being completed by the *nouveaux riches*. The serene eighteenth-century elegance of houses like Weston Park, Lucy Bridgeman's home, began to give way to fantastic Gothic extravagances like Eaton Hall, the seat of the Duke of Westminster, and Harlaxton Manor, home of the Gregory family. Existing houses, such as Highclere and Shadwell Park, were often given merciless face-lifts to bring them into keeping with the new fashion. 'You will, I think,' wrote the Dowager Lady Buxton of her old home in 1858, 'be astonished when you see poor, dear Shadwell again.' It had disappeared in a mass of towers and pinnacles.

Developments in fashion and style are also captured by the camera; for example, it would be hard to find anything truer to the feel of the 1930s than the photograph taken at Kilruddery, county Wicklow (see page 201). The changing times are reflected in the effects that new inventions had upon country house life. That of the motor car, for example, introduced a new type of servant into the household, the chauffeur, and brought about the advent of the weekend. This in turn led to a completely new kind of guest joining the country house circuit, perhaps from the world of show business or sport, and invited in town on the spur of the moment.

As movement from country to country became easier, it was not uncommon to find house-parties filled with visitors from abroad: princes from India, princesses from Germany and millionaires from America decorate the pages of many a family album. American girls, such as Consuelo Vanderbilt who became the Duchess of Marlborough, often ended up marrying into great English families, frequently thereby saving the family fortune, and therefore the family home. Marrying into the rich and powerful middle classes, either at home or across the water, in order to consolidate their fortune, was just one aspect of the ability of country house owners to adapt to the changing times. It was this ability that allowed so many of them to survive with comparative strength for so long.

An early country house photographer, identity unknown.

ON A MAY MORNING in 1851, in Hyde Park, Queen Victoria opened the Great Exhibition, a 'Peace Festival', as she described it, which united the industry of all nations of the earth'. It was housed in a vast, three-tiered, glass winter palace – the 'Crystal Palace', as it was dubbed by Douglas Jerrold in *Punch* – designed by Joseph Paxton, head gardener to the 6th Duke of Devonshire, and it represented one of the peaks of the Victorian era. This exhibition was a celebration of every achievement of the age across the globe, and the crowds gazed in awe at the locomotives of Stephenson and the engineering marvels of Brunel. Amongst the many new inventions at which they wondered was that of photography.

Never before had so many people come so far to visit one exhibition, and at times it seemed as if the whole of England thronged the streets of London. It would therefore be no idle speculation to suggest that amongst these visitors were Lady Lucy Bridgeman and her family, and that it was at this Great Exhibition that she too was first introduced to photography. Whatever the truth may be, it was in the early 1850s that Lucy took possession of her first photographic outfit and began her experiments at Weston Park. The results were kept in a small book by her sister, Charlotte. It is clear that, to begin with, Lucy faced similar problems to those later encountered by Julia Margaret Cameron, who wrote of her first efforts at photography, 'I did not know where to place my dark box, how to focus my sitter, and my first picture I effaced to my consternation by rubbing my hand over the filmy side of the glass.' The early prints are badly stained, and the images often barely discernible. It must be remembered that as yet there was no tradition in photography. There were a number of books available to give some sort of guidance, but the directions given were usually of a very general nature, and many vital points were left to the interpretation or even imagination of the reader. That Lucy was a fast learner is clear, however, from the fact that her failures very soon gave way to successes such as the beautiful study of the servants at Weston.

To these servants who acted as guinea pigs for their mistress's first experiments, photography, as it did to many at the time, must have seemed like magic. Indeed it was not uncommon for people to hold what seem to us absurd ideas about the process. Max Dauthendy, the son of a very popular early photographer, recalled that 'some people believed that my father wanted to collect the sunlight for the purpose of making gold; others imagined that healing powers emanated from the camera which may cure certain diseases. . .'. Another photographer was asked to assure one sitter that there was no danger of his being poisoned by the various vapours in which he would have to be 'enveloped', while an anxious mother asked whether her child could stand the strain of 'being exposed to the rays of the camera for such a long time'.

The photographs with which Lucy followed up those of the servants at Weston, such as the studies of her brother and sister-in-law, Lord and Lady Newport, and their children, and her brother-in-law, Robert Windsor-Clive, very much reflect the new role that the country house had assumed since the accession of Queen Victoria: that of the family home. Houses were now designed or adapted with children as well as husband and wife in mind. Before the nineteenth century, scarcely any attention had been paid to their existence when it came to the planning of a country house; rooms were provided for them, usually on the top floor, but there was little acknowledgement of the fact that they were supposed to be rooms for children. Now, in the new houses that began to appear, there were family wings with nurseries and schoolrooms that were deliberately located close to the rooms of the parents. This family atmosphere is revealed in the early photographs of parents and their children which do little to confirm the traditional idea of the stern and terrifying Victorian paterfamilias; on the contrary, fathers are seen holding their children's hands, and with babies perched upon their laps.

As nineteenth-century families tended to be large, the owner of a grand country house often found himself in the position of having to entertain numerous less well-off relations. The system of primogeniture left countless younger sons in a precarious financial position, and, unless they had been lucky enough to marry an heiress, which was a rare occurrence as they were usually reserved for eldest sons, they invariably ended up in one of the few professions considered suitable for a gentleman, such as the army, the clergy or the diplomatic service. The country houses of their elder brothers, their relations and rich friends provided them with the perfect place to spend their holidays. Admiral Montague, for example, whose mother was a Paget, remembers that their house in Uxbridge was filled with 'numberless uncles and aunts . . . some were half-aunts and half-uncles . . . and to his goodly array were added more numerous progeny until to my juvenile mind the world seemed to consist of nothing but Pagets'. Endless country house albums are filled with the photographs of similar regiments of distantly-related guests.

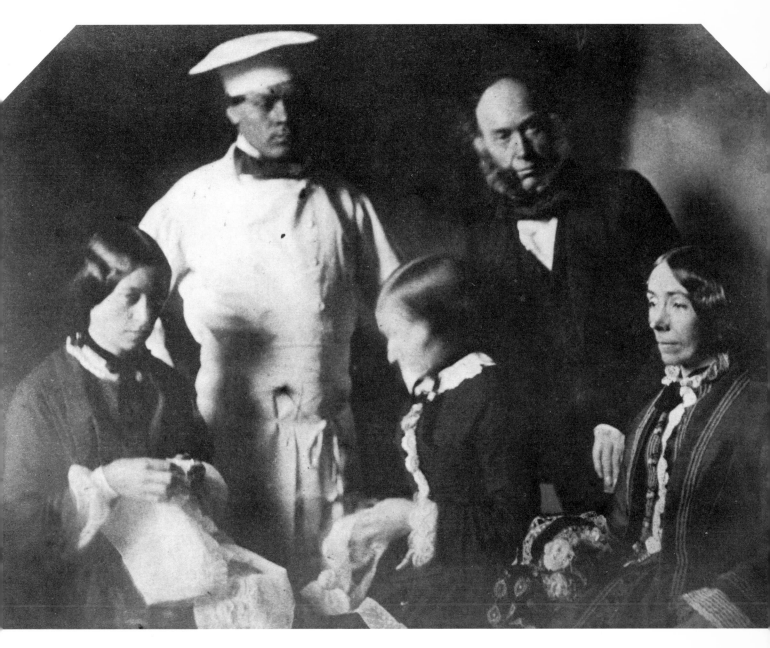

*The servants at Weston Park, by Lady Lucy Bridgeman.
Left to right Lucy Thompson, Harriman, unknown,
Davies, Mrs Austin. From the information given in the 1851
census, it appears that 'Mrs' before a female servant's
name did not necessarily mean that she was married; it was
sometimes used as a courtesy title.*

Below left Lord Henry Lennox, later 6th Duke of
Richmond, photographed at his home, Goodwood
House.

Below right The head keeper at Powis Castle, home of the
Earl of Powis, by Lady Lucy Bridgeman.

Right Henry George, 4th Earl Bathurst.

Above Lady Newport and her children at Davenport House, Shropshire, home of the Davenport family. *Left to right* Gerald, Thomas, Rowland, George and Lady Newport.

Opposite Lucy Bridgeman's brother-in-law, Robert Windsor-Clive, and his daughter Gina. He is wearing a type of hat called a 'wide-awake', which had its origins in a revolt against the top hat in the early 1850s by artists, poets, musicians and other 'bohemians' who took to wearing this wide-brimmed soft felt hat with a low crown.

Left The Marchioness of Lansdowne, wife of the 3rd Marquess, and one of her children.

Below An unknown mother and child.

Opposite Lady Emily Craven, on the steps of her family's house, Combe Abbey, Warwickshire.

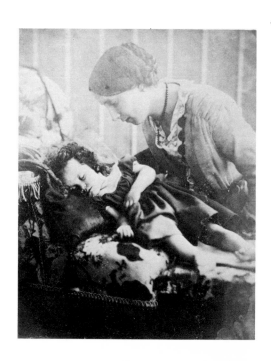

Left A group on the steps of Lord Palmerston's house, Broadlands, Hampshire, taken by Lady Jocelyn in 1858, two years before Palmerston (*centre*) became prime minister.

———

Below A group at St Leonards-on-Sea, Sussex, by Lady Jocelyn.

Traditionally, people had gone to the seaside for their health. Brighton, for example, had long been a fashionable and exclusive health resort, as had Weymouth, ever since 1788 when George III had gone there to recuperate from his illness and had bathed from a machine painted to look like the Union Jack. Now the seaside became a place for holidays, and all round the coast little fishing villages grew into resorts. Amongst the most popular were Ramsgate, Pegwell Bay, Broadstairs, Margate and Weston-Super-Mare; and after Queen Victoria had her first dip on 30 July 1847 in Osborne Bay, from her own larger than usual bathing machine, the Isle of Wight, in particular Ventnor and Ryde, became fashionable.

Above Lady Charlotte Bridgeman, photographed by her sister Lucy at the front entrance to Castle Bromwich.

———

Opposite Lord Newport, eldest son of the 2nd Earl of Bradford and brother of Lucy Bridgeman, and his wife, photographed by Lucy at Castle Bromwich, the dower house of Weston Park. Lucy often signed her pictures, in this case in the bottom right of the photograph, with her initials L and C, either side of the B of her surname.

Below Sir George Wombwell holds the reins of his family's coach at Newborough, his house in Yorkshire. The gentleman in the white hat is Viscount Courtney, later Earl of Devon. It was in coaches such as this that the aristocracy travelled to and from London for the season.

Opposite top A country house orchestra, possibly at Heaton House, Lancashire, seat of the Earl of Wilton. The lady seated at the front is Lady Katherine Egerton; immediately to the left of her, also seated, and holding a trumpet, is a Mr Mitford; the conductor is Mr S. Egerton.

Opposite bottom Taken at Patshull House in Staffordshire, Lucy Bridgeman entitled this musical group 'Rejoicing after the Fall of Delhi'. This refers to the capture of Delhi by the British on 20 September 1857, after a siege that had lasted since June. The man in the photograph is probably John Bridgeman.

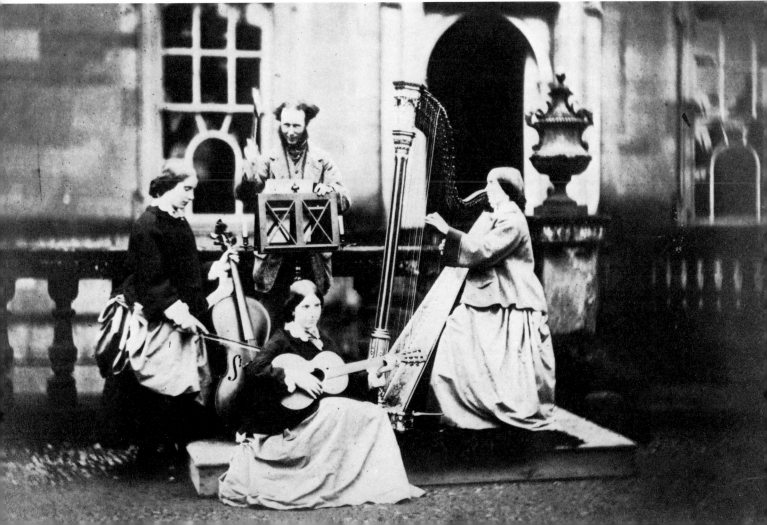

Above Members of Lord Suffolk's family outside Charlton House in Wiltshire.
The ladies are (*left to right*) Lady Isabel Atherly, Lady Suffolk, Lady
Westmorland and Lady Mary Howard.

Left The conservatory at Weston Park by Lucy Bridgeman. *Left to right*
Unknown, John Bridgeman, Lady Charlotte Bridgeman. Conservatories were
first built in the nineteenth century; as indoor gardens, they represented a
growing interest and delight in plants which also encouraged the introduction
of flowers into the house in vases and pots.

Above The splendid first-floor gallery of Adare Manor, Lord Dunraven's house in county Limerick, is 132 feet long, with Willement stained glass and re-erected woodwork from the Low Countries. This interior shot is extraordinary for the detail it manages to capture in the days before electric lighting. It was probably taken by H. A. Herbert of Muckross Abbey, county Kerry, and presents us with a perfect period conversation piece of a family at home in a great house.

Right The drawing-room at Broadlands, Lord Palmerston's house, by Lady Jocelyn.

Above The garden at Panshanger, home of the Cowper family.

———

Opposite Members of the Bagwell family gathered on the lawn of Marlfield House, county Tipperary, to play archery, a popular country house sport at the time. This photograph was taken by Samuel Hemple, who included it in what he claimed was the second earliest book integrating text and photographs, after Piazzi Smyth's *Tenerife*.

———

Previous page The avenue at Helmingham, home of the Tollemache family in Suffolk.

1860/1869

WITH THE DAWNING of the 1860s the country house was fast approaching its heyday, with house-parties becoming more and more fashionable, and, consequently, an ever-increasing circle of guests. It was an influx that most country houses were well able to cope with, and new ones were planned with it in mind. A ground floor with eight large rooms was not exceptional; these usually included a drawing room, library and dining room, a breakfast room, a morning room, a study for the master and a boudoir for his wife, and a billiard room. The last was exclusively the domain of the male members of the party, and some houses also had a smoking room for their use. The ladies' territory was considered to be the drawing and morning rooms, although gentlemen were allowed to enter these if they so wished, while the reverse applied to the library. In addition, some houses incorporated exceptionally large rooms such as the great gallery at Adare Manor, which is one hundred and thirty-two feet long, and a revival of similar medieval and Elizabethan rooms. Here the house-party could congregate in one place either before meals, or for games such as charades or amateur theatricals, both of which were fashionable pastimes. As far as sleeping accommodation was concerned, twenty to thirty bed-rooms were quite normal, the bachelors and unmarried ladies kept strictly apart on separate corridors.

With houses now geared to constant entertainment on a lavish scale, large numbers of servants were required. Unlike in the seventeenth and eighteenth centuries when the sleeping quarters for servants were either on the top floor of the house, or in the kitchen, or even over the stables, most houses now incorporated a special servants' wing whose design was as elaborate and complex as the rest of the house. This was not just because of the large numbers of people involved – less than ten servants was a rarity in a country house, while grand houses like Eaton Hall had up to fifty – but because of the equally complex hierarchy of servant life. The photographs of the servants at Petworth provide a perfect example of the servant population of a great house.

Their departments were divided into four: the butler's, the housekeeper's, the cook's and the laundry maids'. The butler's department was all-male while the rest, except possibly for a chef in charge of the kitchen, were entirely female, and, other than in the servants' hall which was neutral ground, it was thought best that, wherever possible, they should be kept apart. Their sleeping accommodation therefore had separate staircases. This did not mean however that marriage between servants was unknown. At Petworth, for example, the 1st Lord Egremont's valet, Owen, married Mrs Wyndham's maid, Thomas.

The hierarchy 'below stairs' was strict. In a grand house the most important of the servants – the butler, the head cook, the housekeeper, the senior ladies' maids and valets, the head gardener, the coachman, and visiting servants of equal rank – took their meals together in a separate room off the servants' hall. They were served by a footman or pantry boy. In a smaller country house, the upper servants were entertained by the housekeeper. At Petworth, apart from overseeing the cleaning of the house and such duties as the preparation of linen for the bedrooms, the housekeeper Mrs Smith, who was in command of all the housemaids, was responsible for the provision of such things as tea, coffee and sugar. She was also in charge of a stillroom where cakes were baked.

The domain of Mr Dine, the butler, formerly first Groom of the Chambers, was his pantry where he ruled over the footmen and other indoor male servants. His main duties were the care of the plate and glass, the table linen, the wine cellar and the arrangement of the table. Next to his pantry were a variety of small rooms in which footmen or odd men, such as Moore, brushed and cleaned clothes and shoes, sharpened and polished knives, looked after the oil lamps and candles, and performed diverse other tasks.

The kitchens of a country house were often on a vast scale, having, as Robert Kerr wrote in *The Gentleman's House*, 'the character of a complicated laboratory, surrounded by numerous accessories specially contrived in respect of disposition, arrangement and fittings, for the administration of the culinary art in all its professional details'. At Petworth, not unusual in a grand house, Lord Egremont had a French chef, Monsieur Baubbit, who would have ruled over an army of cooks, scullerymaids and dairy maids. Beyond the kitchens was a maze of rooms that included a scullery, pantry, larders for meat, game and fish, a dairy and a dairy scullery. The laundry, wash house and ironing room, at Petworth under the supervision of Reynolds, the head laundry maid, was usually completely independent from the rest of the house, and not under the control of the housekeeper. They also had a brewery at Petworth, run by Mr Davis, though by the end of the 1860s this was becoming less common in country houses.

'*Acre, Boro and Tweety*'. Tweety was Theresa Augusta Tighe
of Rossana, county Wicklow, and here she is leaning against the
doorway of the Croftons' photograph house at Mote Park. In
1864 she married her cousin, Charles St George Crofton.

Above William Thomas Horner, 4th Earl of Ilchester, and his wife Sophia Penelope. He was a distinguished diplomat, and in 1835 was appointed Under Secretary of State for Foreign Affairs. He is the embodiment of the words of R. H. Emerson who, when commenting on the way the Englishman dressed, wrote, 'If he is a lord he dresses a little worse than a commoner.'

Right A family group at Powderham Castle, Devon. *Left to right, standing* The Rev. and Hon. C. L. Courtney, Lady Agnes Courtney, the Earl of Devon and Miss Minna Fortescue; *seated* Lady Caroline Courtney and the Countess of Devon.

Right and opposite The Prince and Princess of Wales (later Edward VII and Queen Alexandra) outside Abergeldie Lodge in Scotland, August 1863.

These two photographs were taken exactly a year after the Prince had proposed to Alexandra. One of the first people with whom he chose to share his news was his close friend, Charles Lindley Wood. 'I keep my promise,' he wrote to him from Brussels on 10 September 1862, 'and send you a few lines to tell you the *all* important has arrived; I proposed to the young Princess yesterday out walking and I was immediately accepted, and I can assure you that I now feel the happiest of mortals. The two days before were rather nervous ones for both of us, though I think the Princess knew what was coming. I only hope that some day you may also be as happy as I am. . . .'

Opposite Lieutenant
General Sir James
Lindsay and his
grandson, Ludovic,
later 26th Earl of
Crawford and 9th Earl
of Balcarres, who was
destined to have a
remarkable career
which included the
creation of one of
the world's finest
collections of rare
books. He was also a
brilliant astronomer,
and by the age of thirty
was President of the
Royal Astronomical
Society and a Fellow
and Vice-President of
the Royal Society.
Added to this he was,
with the help of the
young Italian engineer
Sebastian de Ferranti, a
pioneer in electricity
and radio.

Above Lord and Lady
Fitzhardinge with two
of their grandchildren,
Evelyn and Ella
Gifford. The
Fitzhardinges lived at
Berkeley Castle. He
was Liberal MP for
Gloucester in six
Parliaments.

Left Lord Buckhurst
and his baby son. He
was Reginald Windsor
Sackville-West, later
Earl de la Warr. His
wife was Constance,
first daughter of Lord
Lamington.

Top left Mr R. Balfour, dressed for a walking tour. *Top right* Lord Chesterfield, wearing a 'Tweedside', an easy-fitting country suit of Scottish design.

Above left Lord Stanhope and Sir Henry des Voeux. Sir Henry is wearing the English gentleman's uniform, the black silk hat and frock-coat of cloth. *Above right* Lord Coventry and Admiral Rouse, the former sporting the new shorter top hat which came into fashion in about 1866.

Top left Lord Burghersh in fancy dress. *Top right* The Duchess of Manchester's children.

Above left Lady Suffield's children. *Above right* Reginald and James Duncombe, the sons of the 1st Earl of Feversham.

Above 'Mr Charles Manners'.

Opposite Lady Alice and Lady Katherine Thynne,
daughters of the Marquess of Bath.

Above, left to right Orlando, Helena (in pram), Margaret and Beatrice Bridgeman.

Left The ladies Bridgeman, cousins of Lady Lucy.

Right The unfortunate-looking child on the pony is John Maxse, eldest son of Sir Ivor Maxse who married Mary Wyndham, daughter of the 2nd Lord Leconfield. The photograph was taken at Petworth.

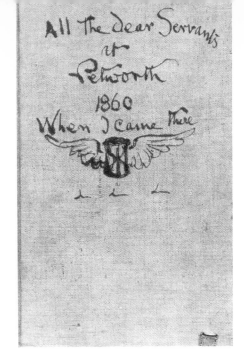

The following series of photographs of the servants at Petworth was collected together and captioned by Mrs Percy Wyndham, wife of Percy Scawen Wyndham, the second son of the 1st Baron Leconfield. They were married on 16 October 1860, and spent much of the first few years of their married life at Petworth. The captions below and overleaf are the original ones written by Mrs Wyndham.

Top row, left to right The Under-Butler at Petworth (sitting); the other cannot identify. May be Moore, an old Odd man/Shepherd, Huntsman for years under first and second Lord Leconfield/*Dear* old Bowler, nurse to Percy and Constance Wyndham at Drove and Petworth. Afterwards became a monthly nurse and attended all the family, Lady Mayo, Mrs Mure, and myself, Lady Munster, and many others/Thomas maid to Mrs Percy Wyndham; married Owen, first Lord Egremont's valet/Mr Sherwin, head keeper. Lived at lodge at top of park near the deer paddock/Reynolds, Laundry-Maid.

Middle row, left to right George Dilloway, Park Keeper at the Turkey Lodge who hunted the pack of Clumber spaniels/Jones, head gardener at Petworth for several years. Went to be head gardener in the Queen's garden at Windsor, and died in her service/Damon, Keeper of the Stallions from Lord Egremont's time. He tended Whalebone all his time/Servant for a short while at Petworth, cannot remember his name/Mr Smith, Bailiff and manager of the home farm at Stag Park/Phillips, for many years Lord Leconfield's coachman.

Bottom row, left to right A butler or under-butler (name forgot) who was at Petworth (not for very long) in the later days/Mrs Smith, housekeeper, formerly Mrs Lingford/Davis, Brewer/Redmond, for many years Lord Leconfield's Pad Groom/Owen, Lord Leconfield's valet. Married Thomas/Mr Baubitt, French Cook at Petworth for numbers of years.

Mrs Bragg, Lady Leconfield's maid, remained on at Petworth after her ladyship's death, in 1883. She had also nursed Lord Leconfield until his death in 1869/Mr Upton, Clerk of the Works, Petworth/Gibson, Stud Groom at Petworth for many years.

Mr Dine. First Groom of the Chambers and then Butler for many years at Petworth, nearly all the time (if not all) we lived there/Mr Haywood, for many years Bailiff and land valuer. A Baptist, died at a great age. An honest able man/One of the keepers, perhaps Steer.

Mr Peter Smith (who married Mrs Lingford), Bailiff. He was a Cumberland man and was called Cumberland Smith to distinguish him from Smith of Stag Park/Adsett, keeper at North chapel. (Could not read or write, and consequently was the only one who could say correctly how many birds he had reared.)/Mrs Greenfield, Dairy Maid.

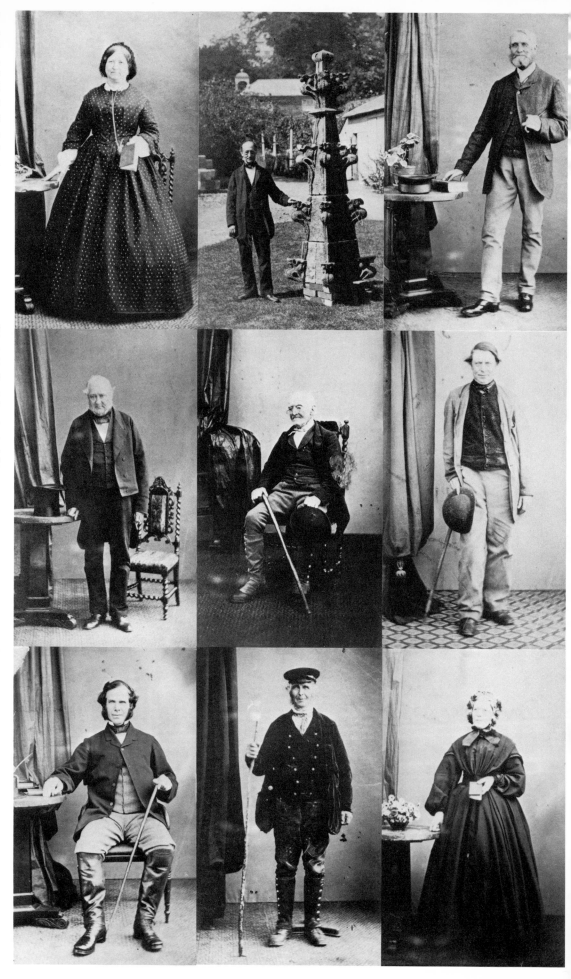

Above The drying and ironing-room of the Petworth laundry. The flat-irons are all laid out on the black cast-iron range on the left. The hot pipes coming out of the range run up the walls and along the ceiling of the laundry, from where the washing is hanging on huge wooden racks. The washing was done in a separate room. Country house laundries were generally completely independent of the running of the main house.

Below The Hon. and Reverend Sidney Meade and Mrs Meade, at Wilton House, Wiltshire, seat of the Earl of Pembroke.

Below A group at Wilton. *Left to right* Mr Hubert Parry, Lady Adine Murray and Lady Maude Herbert. Lady Maude was the second daughter of Sidney, 1st Baron Herbert of Lea, who himself was the fourth son of the 11th Earl of Pembroke. She later married Mr Hubert Parry, by which time he was Sir Hubert Parry, 1st Baronet, of Higham Court, Gloucester.

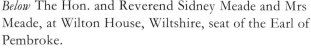

Wilton is one of the oldest boroughs in England. King Alfred established an abbey there in 871, on the site of the present house. When this was dissolved in 1544, the lands were given to William Herbert, 1st Earl of Pembroke, by Henry VIII. Here, possibly basing it on designs by the court painter Hans Holbein, he built Wilton House. The 2nd Earl of Pembroke married Mary, the sister of Sir Philip Sidney; she was famous as a patron of poets and men of letters, and, in collaboration with her brother, she translated the Psalms in metre. Edmund Spenser, Ben Jonson and Marlowe all visited Wilton under her rule, and it is possible that Shakespeare played there. After a major fire in 1647, the house was redesigned by Inigo Jones and his son-in-law John Webb; later alterations were made in 1800 by James Wyatt.

Left Lady Maude Herbert.

Opposite Miss Alice and Mr Francis Blunt. The brother and sister of the poet Wilfrid Scawen Blunt, they both died of tuberculosis.

Right Miss May Lindsay and Lieutenant General Sir James Lindsay, a cousin of hers through her grandfather. She was the aunt of Ludovic, 26th Earl of Crawford, who appears on page 50.

The Palladian bridge which spans the river Nadder in the park at Wilton
was designed by Henry, 9th Earl of Pembroke, with the assistance of his
clerk of the works, Roger Morris. It was completed in 1837. Two years
later, his scheme for the building of a new bridge over the Thames bore
fruit when he laid the first stone of the old Westminster Bridge, work on
which he supervised for the next eleven years.

The Bathurst boys are probably the sons of the 6th Earl Bathurst of
Cirencester Park. The Herbert boys are the sons of Sidney, 1st Baron
Herbert of Lea; though we do not know which is which, they are
George Robert Charles, 13th Earl, Sidney, 14th Earl, William Reginald,
who was lost at sea aboard HMS *Captain* on 6 September 1870, and
Michael Henry.

Above and overleaf *Three collages from an album kept by Miss Harriet Moncrieffe.*

———

Opposite *An extraordinary collage from the album of H. A. Herbert of Muckross Abbey, county Kerry. It is annotated as follows:*
1. Marchioness of Hastings. 2. Duchess of Montrose. 3. Lady Fitzgerald. 4. Countess of Shannon.
5. Countess of Donoughmore. 6. Duchess of Wellington. 7. Lady Emily Peel. 8. Madame de Persigny.

Cricket Group enjoying at the departure of Lady Alice Gaisford.

The 1860s were really the heyday of country house
cricket. H. D. G. Leveson-Gower, the famous
cricketer, described what for him was the ideal
week of country house cricket: 'People are asked to
stay in the house who are all previously acquainted
with one another, thereby removing any stiffness or
undue formality. I do like a hostess to act as mother
to the team, and for the old sportsman who
entertains us to stand as umpire. A bevy of nice
girls is needed to keep us all civilised, and the
merriment is then tremendous. . . . Anyhow there is
a dance one night. On the others, songs, games,
practical jokes, any amount of happy, innocent
nonsense, as well as perhaps a flirtation. . . . The
cricket itself ought to be of sufficient importance
to interest everybody, but not be allowed to
degenerate into an infatuation, and therefore a
nuisance to the fair sex. . . . As for the cricket
lunches . . . champagne lunches are being horribly
overdone. Men do not play good cricket on Perrier
Jouet, followed by Crème de Menthe, with two big
cigars topping a rich and succulent menu. No, give
us some big pies, cold chicken, a fine sirloin of
English beef, and a round of brawn, washed down
by good ale and luscious shandygaff. That is all
cricketers want, and kings only fare worse.'

1860.12. Windsor.

Colonel Heneage. Colonel Goodlake. Lord Skelmersdale. Colonel F. Bathurst.
Colonel Hon.ble F. Berkeley. Mr. I.L. Baldwin. Lords Berkeley and Henry Paget.

Mr. Harvey Fellowes. Mr. Dyke. Mr. O. Twiss. Colonel F. Marshall. Capt. Lambert. Mr. S. Mordaunt. R. Marsham. Capt. Marshall. Marq.ss of Anglesey.
Captain Barnett. Mr. A. Balfour. War.n of Hastings. Mr. F. Norman. Mr. R.A. Fitzgerald. Lord H. Paget. Mr. H. Marshall. Capt. for Kent.

Canterbury 1861.

Below A group of four ladies at Westerdale. *Left to right*
'The Hon. Mrs H. Campbell, Blanche, Emily, Lady C.'.

Opposite top A game of croquet at Castle Bromwich.
Left to right Lord Grey de Wilton, Lady Newport,
Lord Newport, Miss Bridgeman, Lady Grey de Wilton,
Miss Anson and Mr Bridgeman.

Opposite bottom Lady Alice Egerton, Lady Elizabeth de
Ros and Lady Katherine Egerton play on a makeshift
see-saw, possibly at Egerton Lodge.

Above A series of still lifes of dead game by an unknown photographer. These studies, which have a macabre beauty, were made at a time when shooting was becoming increasingly popular as a sport, chiefly owing to the Prince of Wales's influence.

———

Opposite top '1st stag of the season', shot by H. A. Herbert of Muckross Abbey.

Opposite bottom A shooting party gathered on the steps of Warter Priory, shipping magnate Charles Henry Wilson's house in Yorkshire. *Left to right* 'Lord G.', Mr Hamilton, Miss L'Estrange, Mrs Ffolliot, Mary L'Estrange (with dog), Mr Ffolliot, Lady Muncaster (also with dog), Mr Player, Lord Muncaster, keeper.

Right A beautifully composed informal group on the lawn at Calwich Abbey, Staffordshire, home of the Hon. Augustus Duncombe.

Below The Rectory Garden at Wimpole, Cambridgeshire, in 1865, then home of the Earl of Hardwicke and his family (the Yorkes). *Left to right* Mrs Joseph Yorke, who appears to be sitting at an early sewing-machine, Mrs Currie, Joseph Yorke (standing at the back), H. Currie (sitting), Campbell Yorke (lying on the ground), the Hon. E. Yorke and Lady Agneta Yorke.

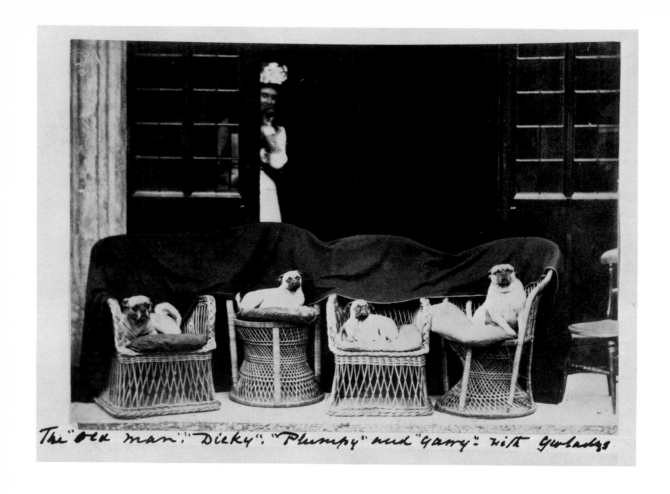

The "old man", "Dicky", "Plumpy" and "Garry": with Gwladys

Above The Herbert pugs posed in the garden at Wilton, with Gwladys Herbert in the background.

Opposite The Marchioness of Hastings and Lady Charles Kerr, surrounded by their pets on the lawn at White Place, near Maidenhead. Florence Hastings had caused a scandal in 1864 when she eloped with Harry Hastings shortly before her intended marriage to Henry Chaplin. This photograph was taken in the summer of 1868 when she had come to White Place to escape from Harry, who was fast on the road to ruin.

1870/1889

Breakfast in an unidentified house, photographed
by the Hon. Hugh Annesley.

B Y THE 1870s there was little variation in the pattern of life enjoyed by a house-party in a large country house. The day began with breakfast which was attended by the entire party and which was, according to a description given by Lady Randolph Churchill of a breakfast at Blenheim on one of her first visits there, almost as formal an affair as dinner. 'When the house was full for a shooting party, even breakfast was made a ceremonious meal, and no one dreamed of beginning until all had assembled. The ladies would be dressed in long velvet or silk trains, and I remember one morning laughing immoderately when Lady Wilton, in appearing in an electric blue velvet, and being asked who made it, said with conscious pride, "It's a Stratton," as one would say "It's a Vandyke."' The meal was served at nine or ten o'clock, and most of the gentlemen in the party would already have been up for an hour or two taking exercise in the park, either walking or riding. This helped prepare them for the massive amounts of food that graced the table and the side table on such an occasion – tea, coffee, chocolate, cold meat, game, fish, sausages, eggs, kidneys, bacon, toast, muffins, butter, marmalade and fruit in season.

When breakfast was over the ladies retired, either to their rooms, all of which would have been furnished with a writing desk, or to the morning room, to read, embroider or write their letters and diaries. For the men there was invariably some kind of sporting activity, of which by far the most popular was shooting. It was a great distinction for a host to lay on a good shoot and to be a good shot, particularly since the Prince of Wales's passion for the sport had made it so fashionable. Men like Lord de Grey, Lord Ripon and Lord Walsingham, the finest shots of their day, set a new standard in the organization of their shoots and the entertaining that went with them. There can be few country house albums that do not bear witness to the Prince of Wales's endless sporting tours. Wherever he went, a photographer would be on hand to record the triumphant party, their game laid out beside them, either in front of the house or in the field.

Of all the great shooting hosts, perhaps the strangest was the Duke of Westminster. In spite of the fact that he was the owner of one of the finest shoots in the country, he never specifically asked people to stay to shoot. Those lucky enough to know the form, however, never failed to arrive with the full paraphernalia of pheasant shooting included in their luggage. Lord Ernest Hamilton recalled how, on the advice of a friend, he dutifully arrived on his first visit to Eaton with his guns, but that there was not a whisper on that first night of any shooting the next day. This appeared to make little difference to most of the male guests who appeared at breakfast fully dressed in knickerbockers and shooting boots. There was still not a word from the Duke about shooting, and after a while the partly dispersed in some despondency of mind to follow other pursuits. 'About half-past ten,' he wrote, 'I was dejectedly smoking a cigarette in the hall, having by that time definitely abandoned all hope of shooting, when the Duke strolled dreamily up to me and said, "Brought a gun?". I replied brightly that I had. "Care to come out and see if we can pick up a pheasant or two?" he continued.' The result of this somewhat nonchalant invitation was the slaughter of a thousand pheasants in the two hours before lunch. 'The Duke never shot after lunch,' continued Lord Ernest, 'but while he was shooting he liked to be busy.'

The ladies joined the party for luncheon which took place either back at the house, or in some grandiose, medieval-style tent, and they might stay out to watch one or two drives in the afternoon. Out of the shooting season there were a variety of other entertainments for the amusement of house-parties. Cricket, for example, was very popular amongst the upper classes and in many houses, Wilton being one, cricket weeks were a regular occurrence. Another game that had become very fashionable since Lord Lonsdale had laid out a lawn was croquet This was particularly attractive as it could be played by women and children as well as men. Tennis, too, was just arriving on the scene, although it was some time before it became as popular as badminton. Those houses with great lakes, such as Castle Howard and Longleat, could also provide boating for their guests, or, where there was a river, fishing. Most women rode and, during the season, the bravest of them went hunting. At the end of the afternoon the whole party would congregate for an elaborate afternoon tea served in the drawing room, or, if the weather was fine, on the lawn.

The climax of the day was dinner which in a great house was a magnificent, if rather heavy, affair with the dining-room table lit by forty or fifty candles, and shining with gold and silver. At grand dinners such as this it was quite normal to have at least thirty dishes served in succession by an army of footmen. Entertainment after dinner very much depended on the particular house. At Belvoir Castle, for example, there was a resident orchestra. 'The band performed every night,' recalled the Earl of Desart, 'and after dinner played a few bars of a quadrille tune, and played no more until some of the party formed up in their places for the dance. It was really very funny. All the guests, ranging in age from sixty or seventy downwards, joined in the quadrille. . . . Afterwards there was a *valse* and a polka for the young people.'

After the ladies had retired to bed the gentlemen donned their smoking jackets and retired to the smoking room for drinks and cigars. In many houses smoking was still considered to be a thoroughly undesirable habit, and these rooms were sometimes well out of the way. At Ickworth, for example, the seat of Lord and Lady Bristol, smoking was confined to 'a sort of bar-parlour, with stone floor and horsehair furniture, that was situated in the sub-hall near the servants' quarters. To this cheerless retreat the gentlemen might repair when they had lit the ladies' candles, and said goodnight to them at the foot of the great staircase.' But as the 1890s approached, smoking came to be more generally accepted, particularly as the Prince of Wales was such a heavy smoker, and this was just one indication of a more relaxed atmosphere in society.

Above A summer house-party grouped around the sculptured fountain at Witley Court in Worcestershire, carved by J. H. Foley as the centre-piece of magnificent formal gardens. Witley Court belonged to the Earl of Dudley, one of the richest men in England, whose wealth came from landed property and iron and coal. The Countess of Dudley (*née* Georgina Moncrieffe) is seated in the centre; the others include several of her children, including her only daughter, Edith (in the boat), her sister Lady Mackenzie (*second from the right*), the Marquess of Bath (*fifth from the right*) and, next to him, Miss Violet Mordaunt, later Marchioness of Bath.

Opposite top Witley Court was completely remodelled for the Earl of Dudley; the whole of the original eighteenth-century building, apart from the Nash portico and the baroque church, was encased in sumptuous Italian Renaissance façades built on a palatial scale.

Opposite bottom Drumlanrig, Ayrshire, seat of the dukes of Buccleuch.

Above A summer house-party at Greystoke Castle, Cumberland, home of Henry Howard. With forty guests staying for a week or so, many of them bringing their own maids and valets, it was not unusual for a household, during a party such as this, to consist of over a hundred people.

Opposite Summer entertainments at Pamflete in Devon, photographed by Beatrice, Countess of Durham. The house belonged to her father, John Bulteel.

Capt Pilkington   Mary   Bessie   Mrs Buller   Effie
Miss G Sotten Symonds   Janie   Miss Sotten Symonds
Addie   Miss G Sotten Symonds

Janie   &   Addie

Above The local hunt meeting on the lawn in front of Clonbrock, county Galway.

Left Lord Elphinstone and the thirty-pound salmon he caught in the river Ness in Scotland.

———

Opposite top Lord Forester, setting out on a shooting expedition from Willey Park, his home in Shropshire. With him are Lady Forester, Miss Seddon and his head keeper.

Opposite bottom A group of keepers at Fenton, Northumberland, photographed by Beatrice, Countess of Durham.

Above and left Boating and tennis at Portnall Park, Surrey. The ladies are the two Miss Gardners, the two Parsons sisters and Lady J. and Lady H. Stewart.

Opposite William Henry Grenfell (*right*), first and last Baron Desborough. He was famous as a sportsman and had played cricket for Harrow, rowed and fenced for Oxford, held the school's record in the mile, climbed the Matterhorn, and won the amateur punting championship. He had also swum across the pool at the bottom of the Niagara Falls. In 1887 he married Ettie Fane, a grand-daughter of the 11th Earl of Westmorland.

Above The Thynne family in an open carriage in front of the steps at Longleat. *Left to right* Alexander (on the steps), a governess, Nanny, Katie, Alice, French (the coachman) and Beatrice.

———

Right John Charles Bengough and his eldest daughter Evelyn Caroline, who was one of ten children. It was probably taken at The Ridge, Wootton-under-Edge, Gloucestershire, the home of the Bengough family.

Above left, left to right Beatrice, Alice and Katie Thynne dressed for riding. They are wearing a fairly new fashion, the slouched felt hat, in preference to the more traditional man's top hat.

Above right Their brother, Viscount Weymouth, the eldest son of the Marquess of Bath, aged seven and already sporting the fashions of the day: a rounded hat or billycock, the ancestor of the modern bowler, a long tweed jacket with narrow lapels, and knickerbockers, in this case tucked into knee-length boots.

———

Opposite John Thynne whispering to his sister Beatrice, known as Queen Bee. Until the age of six, little boys and girls were dressed alike.

Above Constance Olivia Penn, aged seven, with her collection of dolls. Known as Olive, she was the elder daughter of William and Constance Penn of Taverham Hall in Norfolk. They had five children, and her brothers and sisters were Eric, Marjorie, and Geoffrey and Arthur, who were twins. William Penn's father, John Penn, was a famous Victorian engineer who patented a method, still in use today, of lining the sea-bearings of screw propellers with lignum vitae. He was President of the Institute of Mechanical Engineers and a Fellow of the Royal Society.

———

Opposite Four of the nine sons of George Frederick D'Arcy, 2nd Earl of Durham, with their tutor at Lambton Castle. They are (*left to right*) Hedworth, Jack and Freddy (the twins, 3rd and 4th Earls respectively) and Claude.

A seaside group at Pamflete in Devon. *Left to right* 'Mary, Harry Bulteel, Janie, Lilian, Violet, Mrs Bulteel, Mabel, Margaret Baring, Windham Baring, Rowland Baring, Addie, Tina, Lady Baring, Effie'. Beatrice, Countess of Durham, who took this photograph, had twelve brothers and sisters, and her husband, Frederick William, 4th Earl of Durham, also came from a family of thirteen. The Durhams used to visit Pamflete (Beatrice's father's house) for family holidays, and the Violet and Lilian in this picture are their daughters.

Above A Victorian wedding group.

———

Opposite top The hall at Duncombe Park, Viscount Helmsley's seat in Yorkshire, after it had been destroyed by fire in 1879.

Opposite bottom William Reginald, Viscount Helmsley, on his deathbed in 1881. He had died of a fever in Madeira and, although his beard makes him look older, he was only twenty-nine. Photographs such as this were popular in Victorian times, when the mortality rate was high, particularly for children, deathbed pictures of whom are very common.

1890/1899

*The squire of Flintham Hall in Nottinghamshire, captured by the lens of his own panoramic
view camera. These cameras rotated as they photographed, and in this case Mr Hildyard has
peered round the corner, to see if the camera has completed its rotation, a moment too soon.*

THE EARLY 1890s saw a revolution in
photography which had its origins in the
invention of the gelatine dry plate some
twenty years previously. By April 1878 four
British firms were mass-producing these plates, which
could be stored for long periods, and which made possible
truly instantaneous photographs with exposures of a
fraction of a second. They were, however, still made of
glass, and photographers longed for a less heavy and fragile
support. Their wish was granted in 1888 when an American
company started to produce film made of gelatine-covered
celluloid. The real breakthrough which truly popularized
photography came with the introduction by the George
Eastman Company of the first camera incorporating a
roll film. They called it the 'kodak', and it was the
embodiment of simplicity: a wooden box six-and-a-half

inches by three-and-a-half inches by three-and-a-half inches
with a fixed-focus lens giving sharp definition to everything
beyond eight feet, and having only one speed and a fixed
stop. Unskilled amateurs were further encouraged in the
use of this camera by the recommendation of the Eastman
Company that they should return the camera to the factory
for developing and printing. But the real appeal of the
kodak was that suddenly, for the first time, anybody could
photograph who could 'Pull the string – turn the key – press
the button'.

The mass popularity of the kodak which followed
resulted in the 1890s being perhaps the most evocatively
recorded of all decades. Much of this was due to the often
fresh and original approach of the camera's users. The
work of 'The Photographer', who appears on page 119, is
a perfect example of this. Having obviously followed the

advice of an advertisement for the kodak which read 'A collection of pictures may be made to furnish a pictorial history of life as it is lived by the owner, that will grow more valuable every day that passes', he has also taken full advantage of the camera's ability to capture the fleeting moment: Harry Davis and Mrs Margetson in mid-dive; Harry's dog, skulking away from the prying lens. At the same time his photographs have enormous charm – witness 'The portrait of my best friend', which is both simple and touching. As in the work of the great French photographer Jacques Henri Lartigue, the success of these photographs lies in their lack of pretension and great humour.

The fact that the use of the kodak was child's play is shown by the work of a child, Marjorie Penn, for whom her first camera is like a new toy. Her photographs too have a wonderful sense of fun about them. Her sister Olive's hand, clutching a bird, is caught in close-up; her friend Mr Bathurst stands on his head; Olive leaps over a wall and out of the frame in a blur, and her brother Arthur is photographed holding the kodak (by another kodak?).

We now find evidence of a mass of new aristocratic talent, the most outstanding of which must be the work of Beatrice, wife of the 4th Earl of Durham, who lived at Fenton Hall in Northumberland. Her work is remarkable for its quality and composition. It would be hard to find a better example of the ability of photographs to evoke nostalgia than that of her husband and children posing in the long grass in front of Fenton on a summer's day. At Pamflete in North Devon, where the family spent many of their holidays, she also made some extraordinary studies that owe much to the work of Frank Meadow Sutcliffe of Whitby.

Other aristocratic photographers present us with perfect vignettes of the period. Mrs George Fitzwilliam shows us her friend, Arthur Williams-Wynn, taking a lesson in how to ride a bicycle, much against his wish. Lord Alington photographs Mildred Sturt playing with her new kodak. Lord Battersea takes a bizarre study of the child Violet Asquith sitting reading while a dead snake appears to 'crawl' towards her across her cot; and the squire of Flintham Hall, using a panoramic view camera. designed specially for wide-angle photography, and which revolved as it photographed, peers round the corner a fraction of a second too soon to see if the camera has completed its turn, and in so doing captures himself in the wittiest of self-portraits.

The kodak now became an integral part of the country house scene, and young girls began to keep albums in which they pasted their snapshots taken at the various houses they visited alongside the signatures of all the people who had been staying there. These pictorial visitors' books are a fascinating record of the gruelling social circuit of a debutante. For example, this was the schedule of one such young lady, Maud Lyttleton, between October 1897 and February 1898: October 4–9 Hagley Hall (Lord Cobham), Stourbridge; October 12–29 Holkham (Lord Leicester), Norfolk; October 29–30 Ham's (Lord Norton), Birmingham; November 2–6 Shugborough (Lord Lichfield), Stafford; November 6–9 Hawarden Castle (Rt Hon. W. Gladstone), Chester; November 9–11 Eaton Hall (Duke of Westminster), Chester; November 11–20 Saltram (Hon. Montagu Parker), Plympton; November 20–27 Port Eliot (Earl of St Germans), Cornwall; December 7–11 Ashridge (Earl Brownlow), Hertfordshire; December 11–13 Latimer (Lord Chesham), Chesham; December 13–19 Holkham; January 24–28 Althorp (Lord Spencer), Northamptonshire; February 5–9 Madresfield Court (Lord Beauchamp), Malvern.

Above Lady Marjorie Manners, eldest daughter of the Marquess
and Marchioness of Granby, was said to have 'the loveliest eyes
in society'.

———

Opposite Gwendolyn Wilkinson, niece of the 15th Earl of Pembroke.

Above Marion Margaret Violet, Marchioness of Granby, at Sutton Courtney, home of her brother Harry Lindsay and his wife Norah.

Left Violet Granby and her daughter, Marjorie.

These photographs were taken by Violet's brother Harry Lindsay.

Right John Henry Manners, later 9th Duke of Rutland, Robert, Earl of Haddon, his elder brother who died in 1895 at the age of nine, and Marjorie Manners.

Above 'Viola, Diana and Letty', photographed at Haddon Hall, Derbyshire. Viola was the daughter of Sir Herbert Beerbohm Tree; Lady Diana Manners later married Duff Cooper, 1st Viscount Norwich; Lady Violet ('Letty') married Hugo Francis Charteris (known as Ego), eldest son of Hugo, Lord Elcho, and Mary Elcho.

Opposite The Duchess of Portland and Miss Lavinia Drummond at Taplow Court, Berkshire, home of the Grenfell family. Their dresses indicate the popularity at this time of lace, which was used for collars, over-bodices, skirts and, though rarely glimpsed, elaborate petticoats.

Overleaf Violet Asquith, daughter of the future Liberal prime minister Herbert Asquith. In later life she married her father's private secretary Maurice Bonham-Carter, and as Lady Violet Bonham-Carter became famous as a political speaker. This bizarre photograph was taken by Lord Battersea.

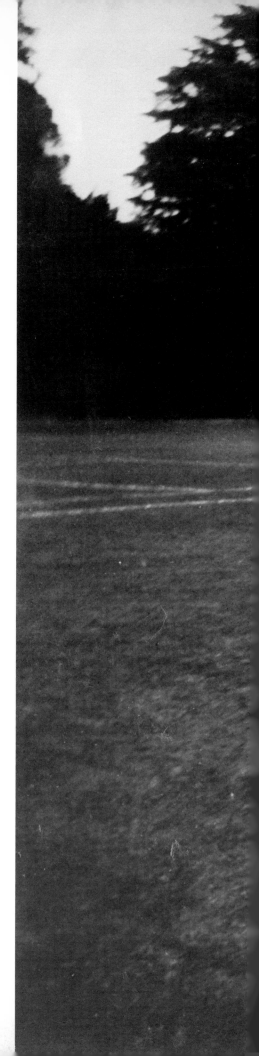

Above and right Arthur Williams-Wynn learning to
ride a bicycle. The photograph was taken at Milton
House, Northamptonshire, by Mrs George Fitzwilliam.
In the 1890s bicycling, which had by then progressed
considerably since the days of the penny farthing,
became all the rage. On Sunday mornings in London,
for example, fashionable people had their bicycles taken
down to Battersea Park by their servants; they then
arrived in their carriages, suitably attired for the
sport, mounted their bicycles and rode solemnly
round and round.

Below Two members of the Hamilton family, cycling at
Hamwood in Ireland.

These photographs from an album kept by the Ashton family reflect
perfectly the new approach to photography that followed the invention of
the Kodak. The instant success of this camera was due, in the words of its
inventor, George Eastman, to the fact that 'anyone who has sufficient
intelligence to point a box straight and press a button could now take a
picture'. The result was that hundreds of ambitious amateurs began to
record the details of their everyday lives, their homes, their friends, their
families, their holidays, often with a charm that makes their photographs
an everlasting pleasure to look at.

The portrait of my best friend.

The Photographer

These beastly photographers
give one no peace.

A quarter to five.

The river is a lazy life.

Summer Days.

Mrs Margetson as the disappearing lady.

The Prince and Princess of Wales at the races, 1898. The Prince loved both the company of racing people and what he called 'the glorious uncertainty of the turf'.

―――――

Overleaf Fenton House, Northumberland, summer 1895. *Left to right* Lilian Lambton, Violet Lambton, Geoffrey, Johnny and Claude Lambton, and Freddy, Earl of Durham. The photograph was taken by Beatrice, Countess of Durham.

Above Elsie and Mab Fitzwilliam, 1898, in a delightful photograph by their aunt, Evelyn Fitzwilliam, wife of the Hon. George Fitzwilliam, second son of the 5th Earl.

———

Opposite top Tea on the lawn at Buckenham Tofts, Norfolk, 1892. *Left to right* R. J. Lucas, Miss Villiers, Mrs W. Penn, Mrs Kerr.

Opposite bottom A tea-party, after tennis, on the lawn at Pamflete, photographed by Beatrice, Countess of Durham. *Left to right* Captain Hughes, Miss Mabel Bulteel, Mrs Bulteel, Captain Tristram, Miss Bulteel, Mrs Bussell and the Earl of Durham.

Left Nanny and members of the Lyttelton family in the nursery at Hagley Hall, Worcestershire.

Below left The schoolroom at Hagley, with the family governess and two of Lord Cobham's daughters.

———

Opposite A family luncheon at Windsor Castle. With the Queen in the Oak Room at Windsor are her daughter and son-in-law, Princess Beatrice and Prince Henry of Battenberg, with three of their children: (*left to right*) Prince Leopold of Battenberg (later Lord Leopold Mountbatten), Prince Alexander of Battenberg (the future Marquess of Carisbrooke) and Princess Victoria Eugenie (later Queen of Spain).

The nursery and schoolroom were where the children of an upper-class family spent the greater part of their lives. In families where the parents were frequently absent, nannies, governesses and tutors could become surrogate parents. The Earl of Dalhousie, for example, whose father, the Governor-General of Canada, failed to recognize his son on his return home, had a tutor 'to whom', he claimed, 'I owe greater obligation than to any man living', whilst Sir Arthur Blackwood admitted that 'the most distinct impression that remains to this day is the personality of dear old nurse'. At the age of eight or nine, most boys were sent off to boarding schools, often harsh and dismal places with long terms and short holidays. The majority of girls were educated at home.

Above left Helen, Viscountess D'Abernon, wife of Edgar, 1st Viscount D'Abernon.

Above right Marjorie Blanche Eva Greville, known as Queenie, daughter of the 5th Earl of Warwick. She was first of all married to Charles William Reginald, Viscount Helmsley and 2nd Earl of Feversham. After he was killed in 1916, she married Sir William Gervase Beckett ('Ger'), brother of the 2nd Baron Grimthorpe.

Opposite Charles William Slingsby, the son of Queenie Helmsley and later 3rd Earl of Feversham.

Above Ethel Priscilla ('Ettie'), Lady Desborough, wife of Willy Grenfell, who became 1st Lord Desborough in 1905, with her sons Billy and Julian. Regarded as one of the outstanding beauties of her day, she was the leader of the 'Souls', a group of young men and women renowned for their brilliance and beauty. It was Lord Charles Beresford who gave this name to the group at a dinner party in 1888, when he said, 'You all sit and talk about each other's souls. I shall call you the Souls.' Other members included Arthur Balfour, George Curzon, George Wyndham, Evan Charteris, Margot Tennant, Hugo and Mary Elcho, and Tommy and Charty Ribblesdale.

Opposite Maud Frederica Elizabeth, Countess Fitzwilliam; wife of the 7th Earl Fitzwilliam, and daughter of the 1st Marquess of Zetland, she was a cousin to Elsie and Mab (see page 128). The two girls are her daughters, Joan and Maud.

Above The Penn twins, Arthur and Geoffrey. Geoffrey was killed in the First World War; Arthur became a Groom-in-Waiting to George VI and later Queen Elizabeth's Private Secretary and Treasurer to the Household.

———

Right Winifred and Lilian Douglas-Pennant at Hagley Hall. In the late 1890s and early 1900s, white was very much in vogue amongst women of all ages. These two fashionable young ladies are also wearing another popular garment of the day, the Russian blouse. Their hats are lingerie bonnets.

Right Lady Elena Wickham. Some twenty years later, in 1917, Lord Warwick wrote: 'I have met ladies who shoot and I have come to the conclusion, being no longer young and a staunch Conservative, that I would prefer them not to.' Other women of this period who shot were the Duchess of Bedford, Princess Radziwill and, one of the best, Mrs Willie Jameson, wife of the millionaire yachtsman who was a close friend of Edward VII; her speciality was driven partridges.

Below Mab Beckett with Kruger and Jester, Gledhow, 1896.

Left 'Ger [Gervase Beckett] and Kruger'.

———

Opposite Two fashion-conscious toffs, Charles and Montagu Spencer, from an Irish country house album.

Above G. Balfour and J. Penn enjoying their shooting lunch at Archerfield, the Duke of Hamilton's house in East Lothian, October 1897.

———

Left Other guests at Archerfield. *Left to right*
Col. Custance, R. J. Lucas, F. E. R. Fryer, F. Penn,
Eric Penn, Basil Kerr.

O.P. clearing the railings

Left 'O.P.' is Olive Penn.
Below Olive, Arthur, Edward and William Penn.
Below left 'Father'.
Below right 'Bathurst' and 'Joan'.

L.Bathurst   Joan

These photographs are from the album of Marjorie Penn, the third child of William and Constance Penn. She never married, and after the Second World War she bought a house in Suffolk with her brother Arthur.

Opposite bottom 'Me' and 'Arthur with the Kodak'.

Family group taken on the eighty-second birthday of the
Dowager Duchess of Abercorn (*seated, centre*) at
Montagu House on 9 July 1894. She had one hundred and
four descendants.

Above This photograph by Beatrice, Countess of Durham, of her family on holiday at Mothercombe beach in North Devon, and the picture opposite, are strongly reminiscent of the work of Frank Meadow Sutcliffe, whose photographs of the fishermen of Whitby and their families were famous. *Left to right* Violet Lambton, Freddy, Lilian Lambton, Miller, unidentified fisherman, Joan Lambton and Mabel Bulteel.

———

Opposite Mabel Bulteel collecting seaweed on Mothercombe beach, 1896.

Left Mildred Sturt and her brand-new Kodak, photographed at Crichel, their home in Dorset, by her father, the 1st Baron Alington. Through her later marriage to Sir Hedworth Meux, the younger brother of the 4th Earl of Durham, she became the sister-in-law of that other keen photographer, Beatrice, Countess of Durham.

Above 'Feo, Miss Daisy de Briener, Mrs L. Drummond'.

Below right 'W. G. Craven, Emmy Kingscote, Mildred'. *Below left* Mildred.

Opposite A group of bathers on the sands near Holker Hall, Cark-in-Cartmel. Lord Richard Cavendish (*standing, second from left*) is wearing the so-called 'regulation university' swimming suit that was, for men, *de rigueur* at the time. Previously they had worn either nothing or possibly short striped trunks. Lady Moyra Cavendish and the girls are fashionably attired in knickerbockers buttoned below the knees, with the upper body clothed in a kind of blouse.

Left A ballooning event near Dublin. At the turn of the century, ballooning was a fashionable sport for both men and women. It reached its peak in 1908 when the balloon meetings at Ranelagh and Hurlingham were like miniature Ascots. The decline of ballooning began in 1909 when Europe first became aware of the aeroplane, and by 1914 the sport had almost disappeared.

1900/1919

WE TWO. 1904

*Mr and Mrs George Fitzwilliam on the lawn at Milton House, Northamptonshire. She is
carrying one of the new lightweight folding cameras. By 1900 it was reckoned that every
tenth person in Britain, that is about four million people, owned a camera.*

FACED WITH THE PROSPECT of a royal visit to
Chatsworth, in 1872 the Duke of Devonshire
wrote to his son Lord Hartington, who was
staying at Sandringham, 'Glad you are
staying at Sandringham, for you will be able to get answers
to several things I want to know. How long do they stay?
How many servants do they bring? How many maids for
the Princess? Do you think they could bring any horses?
Am so afraid that our own may not stand the cheering . . .'
When Edward VII ascended the throne in 1901 the answers
to questions such as these were well known in country
houses all over England. Indeed the cost of entertaining

royalty had already been the undoing of at least two close
friends of Edward's, my great great uncle Christopher
Sykes, and Lord Hardwicke, and now that he was king,
prospective hosts were expected to be even more particular
about the standard of their accommodation. Of the
arrangements for an expected royal visit in 1903, Lady
Londonderry wrote, 'We came to Mount Stewart at
Whitsuntide, and looking over the house . . . the place
looked extraordinarily shabby; and we felt that it must be
tidied up for the great occasion.' This 'tidying up' included
the transformation of the billiard room into an additional
drawing room, the repapering of twelve rooms, the

provision of a specially embroidered upholstery and cushions for the main drawing room, and the complete redecoration in green and yellow silk of the upstairs rooms that were to be the suite of the King and Queen.

Though these expenses may have hurt a few of his friends, on the whole Edward surrounded himself with people who could well afford it. He loved the company of rich men and for many of the *nouveaux riches*, men like W.W. Astor, Colonel John North and J.B. Robinson, his friendship was the gateway to society. This was particularly true of the great Jewish families, like the Rothschilds and the Sassoons, whose inclusion in a house-party would have been unthinkable a few decades previously. Now people began, however reluctantly, to accept them, though their attitude was still very much that of Lucy, the widow of an aristocrat in Vita Sackville-West's novel *The Edwardians*, who, when considering marriage to a Jew, concluded that 'It would be a come-down to marry a Jew, and, physically, Sir Adam was not appetising, but then his millions were fabulous ... besides, Sir Adam could do what he liked with the king.'

Similarly their wealth attracted the king to Americans like Willie and Arthur James, heirs to a great railway and copper-mining fortune, both of whom had married English girls, and who entertained him in the lavish manner which he so enjoyed. The advantages of American riches had in fact long been noted by the English aristocracy, many of whom had married great heiresses to help boost family fortunes that had suffered in the great agricultural depression at the end of the nineteenth century. Miss Minnie Stevens, 'the Belle of Newport', became Lady Paget; Miss Beckwith married the eldest son of Lord Leigh; the beautiful Miss Mary Leiter became Lady Curzon; Miss May Goelet – of whom Daisy, Princess of Pless, wrote, 'How I should hate to be May Goelet, all those odious little Frenchmen, and dozens of others crowding round her millions. An English Duke doesn't crowd around – he merely accepts a millionairess' – was accepted by the Duke of Roxburghe; Miss Consuelo Vanderbilt became Duchess of Marlborough, and there were two American duchesses of Manchester.

The accession of Edward VII thus brought about a considerable change in society, a far greater emancipation stemming from this patronage of the new moneyed class which weakened the snobbery and prejudices of the old guard. This was by no means the only sphere in which his influence was felt. He made several new fashions respectable, including the dinner jacket, which he first wore on a voyage out to India. Following his example, people also started wearing tweed suits, while his love of the Norfolk jacket made it popular throughout the country. This was the beginning of a new and more comfortable era in men's fashion. His patronage of racing, too, made the sport increasingly fashionable with all classes. He loved, as much as the sport itself, to mix with racing people, and soon meetings such as Ascot, Newmarket and Doncaster were important highlights of the season. He won the Derby three times, with Persimmon, Diamond Jubilee and Minoru, and the Grand National with Ambush II. Racing had rarely seen better days.

One of the greatest advances of the Edwardian age was the rapid development of the motor-car, and the subsequent building of a new network of roads. Once again the king made an important contribution to this, as he was one of the earliest motorists in Great Britain. His first experience of motoring was in 1898 during a visit to Warwick Castle where he was given a ride in a six-horse-power Daimler. The following year while staying with Mr and Mrs George Cavendish Bentinck at Highcliffe Castle in Hampshire he was taken out by John Douglas-Scott-Montagu, later 2nd Lord Montagu of Beaulieu, in a twelve-horse-power Daimler which reached the colossal speed of forty miles per hour. He never looked back and, in spite of the fact that in those days motoring was scorned and considered quite unworthy of Royal patronage, by March 1902 he was the owner of several cars, including a Mercedes and a Renault, both painted dark red, and had made a long motor tour in France. It was a pastime that his mother had strongly disapproved of; 'I hope', she told the Master of the Horse, 'you will never allow any of those horrible machines to be used in my stables. I am told they smell exceedingly nasty, and are very shaky and disagreeable conveyances altogether.' It was a sentiment shared by many people.

The advent of the motor-car brought with it its own changes. Families who for generations had been coachmen in the country houses of England now found themselves in the new role of chauffeurs and mechanics. Stables were converted into garages as the coaches made way for gleaming automobiles. The motor tour became a new pastime for the country house set. This new and revolutionary means of transport led inexorably to a faster turnover of guests to the country house, and the eventual establishment of the weekend which was to have its heyday in the 1920s and 1930s.

Edward VII died in May 1910. Two years later, when Lady Desborough held her great fancy-dress ball at Taplow Court, the guests in all their finery might have been forgiven for temporarily casting from their minds the fact that they were all living in cloud-cuckoo land. The last five years had seen a bitterness of quarrelling amongst the British people that was unparalleled since the 1820s and 1830s. The power of the landed classes was being eroded; workers were discovering the power they could wield by striking; and women all over the country were fighting for the vote. There was rebellion in the air. The outbreak of war came with almost perfect timing; it gave all classes the opportunity to work out their frustrations against a common enemy. And even in these inauspicious times, the country house had its uses, for many became a refuge for those lucky enough to have been sent home wounded.

Opposite Lord de Grey, arguably the finest shot of his day, in action at Wilton during a shoot for the Prince of Wales. Lady Randolph Churchill recalled how '. . . once at Panshanger when I was staying with the late Lord Cowper, I saw Lord de Grey shoot in one stand fifty-two birds out of fifty-four, and for a bet this was done with one hand. He had two loaders and three guns.'

Above Shooting at Wilton with the Earl of Pembroke. The Prince and Princess of Wales (later George V and Queen Mary) are standing in the middle of the picture, with the Countess of Pembroke to the left.
Below Another shooting party, this time at Milton with the Fitzwilliams. It includes Lady Elena Wickham (*second from the right*).

Top Hounds crossing the water on an autumn morning.

Above A lawn meet at Wentworth Woodhouse in Yorkshire, seat of the Earl and Countess Fitzwilliam.

Opposite top and bottom A house-party sets off for Doncaster Races from Wentworth Woodhouse, 1903.

Above Miss Muriel Wilson, later Mrs Richard Warde, one of
Edward VII's set who was renowned for organizing amateur
theatricals.

———

Opposite Lady Marjorie Manners, eldest daughter of Henry John
Granby, 8th Duke of Rutland. She and her sisters were known
amongst their friends as the 'Hotbed' or 'Hothouse', an allusion
to a greenhouse, owing to their exotic affectations. She had
many admirers, including the Duke of York and Julian Grenfell,
and in 1912 married the 6th Marquess of Anglesey.

Above Maynard Greville, third son of the 5th Earl of Warwick.

———

Opposite His mother, Frances Evelyn Greville, known as Daisy. A long-standing mistress of Edward VII, and a renowned society hostess in the 1880s and 1890s at whose house-parties at Easton Lodge sexual intrigue ran riot, the Countess of Warwick ended up a confirmed socialist.

Above Mrs Nancy Astor at Cliveden, June 1908. An American by birth, Nancy Langhorne had married Waldorf Astor, later 2nd Viscount Astor, in 1906. They received Cliveden as a wedding gift from his father, William Waldorf Astor, who had bought it from the Duke of Westminster a few years earlier. On becoming mistress of this magnificent Italianate country house, she lost little time in redecorating it to her taste; as she later explained, 'The keynote of the place when I took over was splendid gloom. . . . The place looked better when I had put in books and chintz curtains and covers and flowers.'

———

Opposite Consuelo, Duchess of Marlborough, wife of the 9th Duke of Marlborough. Formerly Consuelo Vanderbilt, daughter of the American multi-millionaire Cornelius Vanderbilt and his socially ambitious wife Alva, she was forced into marriage with the Duke in

1895. The dowry was said to be in the region of two and a half million dollars, and was used to renovate Blenheim Palace. Though the marriage may have brought happiness to Alva, for her daughter it was a disaster. She hated the oppressively gloomy atmosphere of Blenheim, which the 1st Duchess had described as 'that wild, unmerciful house which not even a vast number of feather beds and quilts, all good and sweet feathers, even for the servants, could tame'. She also suffered from a slight deafness, which made entertaining as difficult as her solitary meals with the Duke in the huge echoing dining-room. She was eventually separated from her husband in 1907 and moved to London, where she lived in Sunderland House. Here, freed from the dominating, masculine atmosphere of Blenheim, she became a successful hostess, establishing her own salon with a literary and political flavour. James Barrie declared of her, 'I would stand all day in the street to see Consuelo Marlborough get into her carriage.'

Pickles. *Tom* *Joan*

Above The Fitzwilliam children in their baby-carriages outside Wentworth Woodhouse, 1908.

———

Opposite top Thomas, 2nd Earl of Leicester, aged eighty-eight, photographed in 1908 (he died the following year) at Holkham Hall, Norfolk, with his son, Viscount Coke, his grandson, the Hon. Thomas Coke, and his great-grandson, little Tom. Married twice, first to a Miss Whitbread and then to the Hon. Georgina Cavendish, he was the father of nineteen children, fifteen of whom survived. Thus his youngest son, the Hon. Lovel Coke, at the age of thirteen had a nephew of thirty-four, Viscount Fincastle, and, in the Dowager Lady Powerscourt, a half-sister of sixty-one.

Opposite bottom The Earl of Leicester being carried into Holkham under the careful eye of his butler, on a specially constructed stretcher made after he had suffered, and partly recovered from, a massive heart attack in 1905. After this illness and until his death, his bed was moved into the saloon at Holkham where he used to receive visitors.

Above 'The Picnic', photographed by Mrs George Fitzwilliam. The little boy facing the camera is her son Tom.

Right A fishing expedition, by Mrs George Fitzwilliam. *Left to right* 'Vixen, Mary, Tom, Lady Mary Boyne, Toby'.

Below 'Our picnic on a barge', by Mrs George Fitzwilliam.

Above The Fitzwilliam children on holiday, Seaview, 1902.

Left Children and their nannies grouped around a bathing-machine. The little girl at the front wearing a big floppy hat is Elizabeth Cavendish, later Countess of Salisbury.

Right 'Marion christening *Lavengro*'. The yacht belonged to her father, Gervase Beckett, a director of Becketts Bank and Conservative MP for Scarborough and Whitby, and North Leeds. He was a passionate admirer of George Borrow, and named the yacht after Borrow's book. He later had a second yacht which he also named after a Borrow book, *Romany Rye*.

Below Lavengro under sail.

Right Lavengro in the Caledonian canal.

Opposite top Aboard *Lavengro*, August 1903: Mr West and Dorothy Chandos-Pole.

Opposite bottom 'The Saloon, *Lavengro*'.

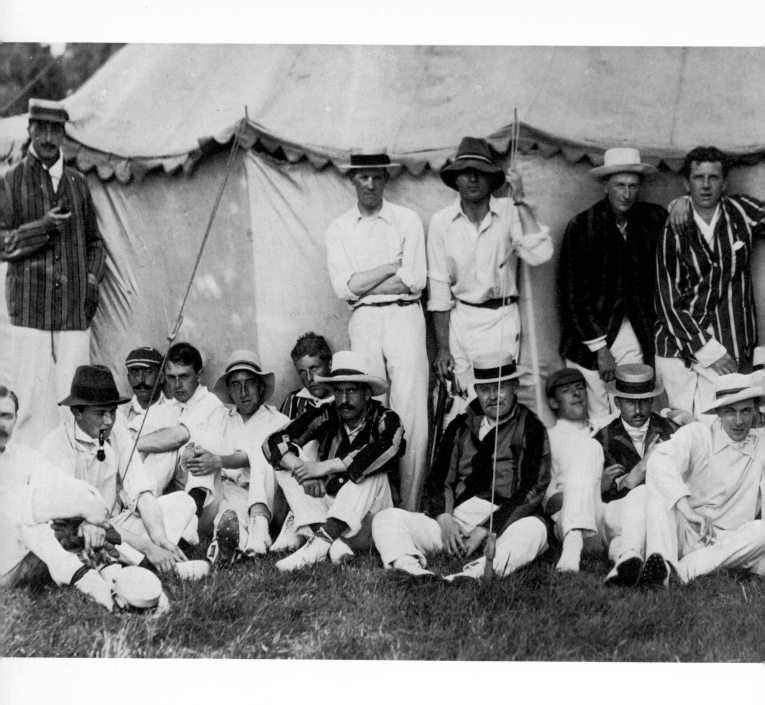

Left A country house cricket group at Honnington Hall, Warwickshire, leased at that time to the banker Howard Gilliat and his family. *Left to right* (standing) 'A. P. Boxall, F. L. Gilliat, C. E. Lambert, C. E. Seymour, Clive Burn, George Buckston, H. O. Peacock'; (sitting) 'Ernest Crawley, Guy Senhouse, C. H. Wild, E. G. Whatley, L. Houghton, Buchanan, Philip Cobbold, A. Cooke, W. I. H. Curwen, G. Drummond, J. F. Gilliat, C. R. Nicholl, R. Fellowes'.

———

Below A summer house-party at Wilton for King Edward VII and Queen Alexandra. *Left to right* (back row) 'Lord Salisbury, Lord Roseberry, Lord R., Charlotte Knollys, Lord Herbert, Commander Forrester, Lord de Grey, Lord Pembroke, the Queen, Lady Pembroke, Lord Durham, V.W., George Herbert, Muriel Herbert'; (front row) 'B.H., Lady Salisbury, Gladys de Grey, the King, Lady Lansdowne, B.W., Lord Lansdowne'.

Above left 'On the road between Grenoble and Chambery'.

Above right A halt to take photographs.

Right Queenie and Ger hold up a mangled inner tube while the chauffeur mends the puncture. Queenie is wearing the traditional costume for motoring which consisted of a flat cap, tied on the head with a thick veil, and a long coat to keep out the dust.

Below Mab and Queenie wait for the car after luncheon.

These four photographs are from a motoring tour of France from 6 May to 30 May, 1913, taken by Gervase and Mab Beckett, and Charlie and Queenie Helmsley. Mab and Charlie were brother and sister, and, unknown to them, her husband Ger and his wife Queenie were already deeply in love when they all went on this holiday together. Fate proved kind to the lovers, though, for within three years of the tour both Mab and Charlie were dead, she of tuberculosis and he of war wounds. Ger and Queenie married in 1917.

H. C. Hoover.

Overleaf William Randal, 11th Earl of Antrim, who was a motoring fanatic, driving his White's Steam Car at Glenarm, his home in Northern Ireland. Known as 'The Buzzard', he was one of ten children, all but one of whom had nicknames given to them by their father, 'The Conjuror'; they were 'Carrie', 'The Grimp', 'The Fox', 'Pom', 'Mabie', 'Cloud', 'Jinny' and 'Mousetrap' (the exception, Hugh, died young). When Carrie, the eldest sister, had children, they were so ugly that they were known as 'Carrie's Monkies'.

―――――――――

Left and below Herbert Clarke Hoover, 31st President of the United States, spent the years between 1902 and 1908 in England. At the time, he was practising engineering, and had a partnership in an English mining company with interests in Cornwall and Derbyshire. He and Mrs Hoover had a flat in Hyde Park Gate in London, and a small country house at Walton-on-Thames called, curiously enough, the White House, which was where they spent their holidays. They both loved motoring, and in his memoirs President Hoover recalled, 'In 1902 we bought our first automobile, a French Panhard. . . . In later years the weekends and holidays of motoring with Mrs Hoover through the English and Scottish counties formed a large part of those stimulating memories which make one forget much of the objectionable conduct of the human animal!'

July 1906 A day at Henley with Hoover.

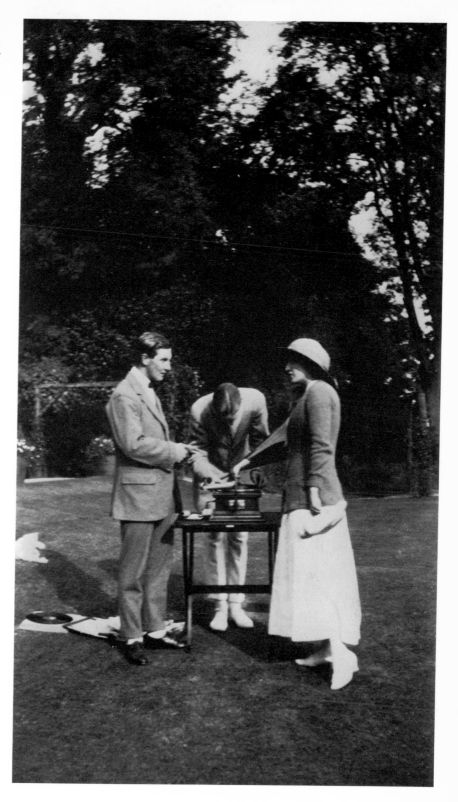

In the couple of years preceding the First World
War, dancing became all the rage: tangos, one-
steps, hesitation waltzes, bostons and turkey-trots
were rushed off the record presses. One of the
largest recording companies, Columbia, even placed
its recording programme under the direction of a
man who danced while the band made the record.
There was an immediate rush to make money from
the growing popularity of the phonograph. In 1912
there were only three manufacturers of the
instrument – Victor, Columbia and Edison; by
1916 there were forty-six.

Above Lady Diana Manners, photographed by a
professional photographer hired by Lady Desborough
for her great fancy-dress ball on 8 January 1912 at
Taplow Court, her husband's family home near
Maidenhead, Berkshire.

Fancy dress was by no means a new pastime for the
upper classes. In the nineteenth century, amateur
theatricals were often the most popular form of
after-dinner entertainment for a house-party, and
many houses, among them Chatsworth, Wargrave
and Blenheim, had their own theatres. The 5th
Marquess of Anglesey, admittedly something of an
eccentric, even used to hire professional actors to
act with him, and turned the chapel at Plas Newydd
into a replica of Sarah Bernhardt's theatre in Paris.
Fancy-dress balls became all the rage after the great
Devonshire House ball, given by the Duke of
Devonshire in 1898. They were to enjoy a

considerable revival in the 1920s when there were
so many that Cecil Beaton remembers it being quite
usual for him not to put on ordinary clothes for a
week or ten days at a stretch.

———

Opposite, top left Lady Rosemary Leveson-Gower and
Miss Monica Grenfell;
top right Lady Joan Capell and the Hon. Francis
Manners;
bottom left Captain Terry and Miss Eva Sawyer;
bottom right The Hon. Ian Hay and the Hon. Victoria
Sackville-West.

Top Wounded officers convalescing at Milton House, Northamptonshire, home of the Earl and Countess Fitzwilliam. During the 1914–1918 war, many country houses were used for this purpose.

Above One of the main rooms at Milton, converted into a hospital ward. In most houses so used, the priceless paintings were removed from the walls.

Opposite top Nurses and wounded soldiers in front of Longleat in Wiltshire, home of the Marquess of Bath.

Opposite bottom Wounded soldiers practise using their crutches.

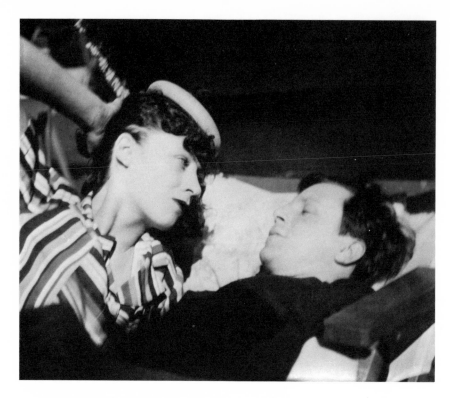

*Lady Caroline Paget and Rex Whistler at Plas Newydd, Isle of Anglesey,
home of the Marquess of Anglesey.*

T HE YEARS FOLLOWING the First World War were marked by various changes in country house life. A combination of factors led to many country houses being run on much less lavish lines. It was far more difficult to get servants. The war had broken what had previously been a secure supply, and had also changed many people's attitude to service. Men who had spent four years fighting in the trenches, on their return did not wish to become butlers and footmen. The country house was also entering the age of the labour-saving device. The vacuum-cleaner, for example, dispensed with the need for so many house-maids. Commercial laundries saw the eventual disappearance of the house laundry. Central heating went a long way to abolishing the endless laying of fires and cleaning of grates. Electric light required only one person to flick a switch, a far cry from the dozens of oil and gas lamps which had to be cleaned and prepared. There were generally more bathrooms, which meant less water to carry, while all kinds of new equipment served to increase efficiency in the kitchen.

All these developments, together with the relaxed post-war atmosphere and the new generation's reaction against convention, led to a far greater degree of informality in country house life. This was the heyday of the country weekend, made possible by the ever-increasing popularity of the motor-car, and it was something of a relief after the long and formal house-parties of Edwardian days. Anyway, during the week most people, young and old alike, were far too busy indulging in the hectic round of post-war revelry. As far as the young were concerned, caution was thrown to the wind as rival groups of what were dubbed 'bright young things' drove around the streets of London at night at break-neck speeds on 'Treasure Hunts', in which the prize usually went to the party with the quickest wits and the most unscrupulous driver. 'Faster, faster! It doesn't matter about the bobby! What's the matter with the car? Step on it!' shouted Duff Cooper as, on one occasion, he made a maniacal attempt to reach the treasure before the Prince of Wales. Every night there were parties, each one attempting to out-do its predecessor with its originality. At one, people came dressed as babies accompanied, where possible, by their former nannies, while at another, given at St George's Swimming Baths, the guests wore bathing costumes and danced around the pool to a negro band. Society bent over backwards to amuse itself.

At weekends country houses received the exhausted revellers, and a new, relaxed kind of house-party evolved. The young broke down the code of snobbery which governed who could be asked and who could not, and suddenly country house albums are filled with photographs of people from the worlds of show business, literature and fashion. The moral code was also freer. In Daisy Warwick's time, while it had been considered acceptable for married people to have affairs (as long as they were never found out), and she would often place those whom she knew to be lovers in adjoining rooms, this was unthinkable behaviour for the unmarried, who were kept strictly segregated. In many houses there was now an end to this rigorous segregation of the bachelors and unmarried ladies, and passage-creeping became an accepted weekend thrill.

Though there was still the formality of lunch and dinner, breakfast had become a quite different affair, with guests helping themselves from a side table and sitting where they pleased. Some of the ladies even had breakfast in bed. As for tea, few bothered to change any more, and it was both informal and moveable. In the summer, picnic lunches were fashionable, and the butler would load up the car with baskets of food and wine for the party to motor off to some local beauty spot, as yet unspoiled by car-parks and litter-bins. Weekend pastimes changed little. In the winter, shooting or hunting; in the summer, tennis, cricket, motoring and croquet. A few houses had the luxury of a swimming-pool. In the evenings there were games: drawing games, acting games, writing games.

New inventions and fashions also had a considerable effect on the lives of the servants in a country house. We have already seen how the chauffeur developed with the invention of the motor-car. The grandest houses now had their own electrician, though in many cases it was the butler who had to learn about fuses and plugs. Added to this, he often had another kind of skill to acquire, for the 1920s and 1930s saw the introduction of the cocktail. Suddenly, in country houses all over England, in the hour before the serving of dinner, butlers could be found in their pantries surrounded by bottles of obscure liqueurs, and fiddling with silver cocktail-shakers of all shapes and sizes (one popular model was in the shape of a fire extinguisher), in a desperate attempt to reproduce the complicated concoctions requested by their masters. In some cases they were more than successful: Cassidy, the butler at Sledmere, my father Sir Richard Sykes's home, was renowned for his 'Sidecars', a mixture of brandy, cointreau and lemon juice, the number of which consumed went some way to reducing the family fortune. There must have been those of the old school, however, who never mastered the art.

The general acceptance of the cocktail was just one example of the influence of America upon fashionable society. This was felt in many quarters, such as fashion and decor, and came about in several ways. The immense and growing popularity of the cinema brought Hollywood taste to the attention of society, as did the influx of American magazines such as *Vogue*. There were also a number of prominent American hostesses who were introducing their ideas, such as Lady Cunard, the former Maud Burke from San Francisco, who entertained at her great town house in Grosvenor Square and her country house, Nevill Holt, in Leicestershire. Her guests included many of the political and literary lions of the day: Lords Oxford, Balfour and Birkenhead, George Moore, the Sitwells and Evelyn Waugh.

Another great hostess was Mrs Ronnie Greville, who liked her weekend parties at Polesden Lacey to contain a mixture of royalty, politicians and the upper echelons of society; guests for one typical weekend, that of 7–9 July 1934, included the King of Greece, Sir Austen and Lady Chamberlain, the Italian Ambassador, Lady Violet Bonham-Carter, the Earl and Countess of Willingdon, and the Earl of Caledon.

But of all the great hosts and hostesses who became famous for their weekend parties in the 1920s and 1930s, without a description of one of which no picture of life between the wars would be complete, undoubtedly the most fascinating was Sir Philip Sassoon. Described by Chips Channon as 'one of the most exciting, tantalising personalities of the age', he had been Unionist MP for Hythe since 1912, was Private Secretary to both Sir Douglas Haig and Lloyd George, and was later Under Secretary for Air. He was immensely rich, and entertained lavishly at his houses Trent Park, Middlesex, and Port Lympne in Kent. 'His hospitality was on an oriental scale,' recalls one of his closest friends, Lord Boothby. 'The summer weekend parties at Trent were unique and in the highest degree enjoyable, but theatrical rather than intimate. He frankly loved success, and you could be sure of finding one or two of the reigning stars of the literary, film, or sporting worlds, in addition to a fair sprinkling of politicians and, on occasion, Royalty.' Lord Boothby, who was a frequent guest of Sir Philip's, goes on to remember '...Winston Churchill arguing over the teacups with Bernard Shaw, Lord Balfour dozing in an armchair, Rex Whistler absorbed in his painting, Osbert Sitwell and Malcolm Bullock laughing in a corner, while Philip himself flitted from group to group, an alert, watchful, influential but unobtrusive stage director, all set against a background of mingled luxury, simplicity and informality, brilliantly contrived. The beautifully proportioned red brick house, the blue bathing pool surrounded by such a profusion of lilies that the scent at night became almost overpowering, the flamingoes and ducks, the banks of exquisite flowers in the drawing room, the red carnation and the cocktail on one's dressing-table before dinner, were each and all perfect of their kind.'

P.J.   Weygand   Foch   H.Wilson   DAVID   P.M.   Philip Kerr   MARSAL   AUSTEN   HANKEY
                                        HERBERT   MILLERAND

188

Opposite At the end of the war, Philip Sassoon was private secretary to Lloyd George, the British prime minister, and he lent his house, Port Lympne in Kent, as the venue for the various Peace Conferences that were then being convened. The first of these took place on 19–21 June 1920; these photographs record who was present. In the bottom picture, the men have been joined by the two hostesses, Sybil, Lady Rocksavage, Philip Sassoon's sister, and Hannah Gubbay, his cousin.

———

Above The second conference, 8 August 1920. The original caption for this reads (*left to right*) Desticker, Evan, Berthelot, [two unidentified] Herbert [the dog], Foch, Lady Essex, Philip Kerr, [one unidentified] Lord Curzon, [one unidentified] Beatty, Millerand, Hankey, Lady Desborough, [one unidentified] Balfour, Lloyd George, Philip Sassoon, Sir H. Wilson [three unidentified].

Right Andrew Bonar Law, David Lloyd George and Austen Chamberlain in private conference. Both Lloyd George (from 1916 to 1922) and Bonar Law (from 1922 to 1923) served as British prime ministers, and each in turn offered the succession to the position to Austen Chamberlain, who refused it.

Left The Duke of York (the future George VI) on the tennis court at Port Lympne.

Below left The Prince of Wales (later Edward VIII), punting with Lady Bridget Coke, with whose sister-in-law Marion he was in love for several years.

Below right The Prince of Wales at Port Lympne.

———

Opposite The Duke and Duchess of York on their honeymoon in 1923, which they spent as guests of Mrs Ronnie Greville at Polesden Lacey.

Elizabeth *Albert*

april 26ᵗʰ — May 7ᵗʰ

Above H. G. Wells plays a careful croquet shot on the lawn at Stanway, home of the Charteris family.

Right Winston Churchill at Port Lympne.

Opposite David Lloyd George at Port Lympne.

P.M.

Above A weekend house-party at Port Lympne. *Left to right* (standing) 'Bob Boothby, Drogo, Loel [Guinness], Rupert'; (sitting) 'Noel Coward, Sybil, self [Philip Sassoon]'.

———

Right Charlie Chaplin at Port Lympne. On his left are Philip Sassoon and his sister Sybil, while Philip Sassoon's cousin, Hannah Gubbay, who often acted as his hostess, sits on Chaplin's right.

Above Elinor Glyn, the Jersey-born romantic novelist, draped across a tiger skin, with which fur she became everlastingly associated after the publication of her notorious novel, *Three Weeks*, in which the young hero is seduced on one by an older woman.

This inspired the famous rhyme:
> *Would you like to sin*
> *With Elinor Glyn*
> *On a tiger skin?*
> *Or would you prefer*
> *To err*
> *Upon some other fur?*

Right (left to right) The Canadian-born film actress, Miss Mary Pickford, Lady Betty Butler and the Duchess of Sutherland at Sutton Place, Surrey, June 1920.

———

Opposite Nancy, Viscountess Astor, Britain's first woman MP. During the late 1930s, at the Astors' country house, Cliveden, she acted as hostess at many gatherings of politicians such as Sir Samuel Hoare and Neville Chamberlain who supported an 'appeasement' policy towards Nazi Germany.

Above and right Sybil, Lady Rocksavage (later Marchioness of
Cholmondeley). The daughter of Sir Edward and Lady Sassoon,
formerly Aline Rothschild, Sybil was a beautiful and brilliant hostess.
She was painted several times by John Singer Sargent, and was dressed
by many of the great designers of the day.

Above Princess Marthe Bibesco. A
Rumanian with splendid red-gold hair, her
exotic looks matched her temperament. One
of the many stories which circulated about
her said that, during the First World War,
the Crown Prince of Saxe Weimar had
promised to spare Paris from bombardment
for love of her green eyes.

Right Taken at Kilruddery in county
Wicklow, this photograph captures
perfectly the fashions of the early 1930s.
Left to right Madame Veronica Fitzgerald
(wife of the Knight of Glin), Lady Maureen
Brabazon, Lady Meriel Howarth and Miss
Fiola Fitzgerald.

Above Sybil Rocksavage and Philip Sassoon
at Port Lympne.

Opposite Lady Diana Cooper (née Manners),
youngest daughter of the Duke and
Duchess of Rutland, with her husband,
Alfred Duff Cooper, later Lord Norwich.

Left The Marquess of Anglesey, whose sister-in-law Lady Diana Cooper had starred in two feature films, *The Glorious Adventure* (1921) and *The Miracle* (1923), was himself a keen amateur movie-maker, and made several films at Plas Newydd using his family and friends as actors.

Below A group of 'bright young things' at Luggala, Ernest Guinness's house in Ireland. *Clockwise, from top* Daphne Vivian, Brian Howard, (one unidentified) and Aileen, Tanis and Maggie Guinness.

Left Brian Howard, one of the original Oxford
aesthetes, photographed imitating a crab by Henry,
9th Viscount Weymouth. A shamelessly affected
homosexual, he was the model for Ambrose Silk in
Evelyn Waugh's *Put Out More Flags*. Waugh never liked
him and, borrowing Lady Caroline Lamb's aphorism
about Byron, wrote that Howard was 'mad, bad and
dangerous to know'.

Below Also at Luggala. *Left to right* Oonagh, Maggie and
Tanis Guinness, Brian Howard, Aileen Guinness and
Daphne Vivian.

Right 'The English Picnic', a photograph by the most fashionable photographer of the period, Cecil Beaton. The cast is (*left to right*) David Herbert, Bridget Parsons, Caroline Paget, Diana Cavendish, Theresa Jungman, Tilly Losch, Tony Herbert, Cecil Beaton, Betty Smith.

A study of F. E. Smith, 1st Earl of Birkenhead, at a picnic. One of the greatest wits of his day, and a brilliant barrister, he became Lord High Chancellor of England. He had an almost boyish sense of fun; one of his favourite tricks was to leap off the side of his yacht with a lighted cigar in his mouth, surfacing with it still alight. Stories of his wit are legendary; one concerned a speech he had made on the subject of old age pensions, in which he commented: 'The death duties are being levied to pay old age pensions. It seems to me a curious thing that one section of the community should live to enjoy five shillings a week, while the other section should have to die to pay them. . . . The Old Age Pension Act provides five shillings a week for a single person and seven and six for a married couple. Note the piety of our government! They give you seven and six a week for living with your own wife, and ten shillings for living with somebody else's.'

Top The Lygon family at Madresfield Court. *Left to right* Dorothy, Mary, Sibell, Lettice, Lady Beauchamp, Lord Beauchamp, William Elmley, Hugh and Richard. The Lygons were close friends of Evelyn Waugh, and Hugh Lygon partly inspired the character of Sebastian Flyte in *Brideshead Revisited*.

Above The Mitford family, Christmas 1925, at Asthall Manor. *Left to right* (standing) Pam, Uncle Jack, Tom, Bertram, 'Muv', Aunt Iris, Nancy; (sitting) Magdalen Bowles, Phyllis Bowles, Diana, Decca, Debo, Unity.

Left The sixteen grandchildren of the 9th Duke of Devonshire. *Left to right* Billy, Arbell, Andrew, Maurice, Pamela, Jean, Carol, David, Michael, John, Judith, Catherine, Elizabeth, John, Anne and Peter.

Left The Knight of Glin in his Peugeot at Brooklands, the motor racing track at Byfleet, Surrey.

Right The Knight of Glin at 101 mph, breaking the lap record at Brooklands when he was working for the Bianchi company, an Italian car firm.

Below Sybil Rocksavage in the new Sunbeam at Port Lympne.

Right Ernest Guinness flying in his Tiger Moth. He was also the owner of a flying boat and two yachts, the 300-ton ketch *Fantome 1* and the 600-ton *Fantome 2*.

Above The Knight of Glin and his aeroplane at Glin Castle in Ireland.

Right Ernest Guinness in the cockpit of a propeller-driven motor boat which he designed. An intrepid inventor, he used to walk around weighted down with scientific instruments.

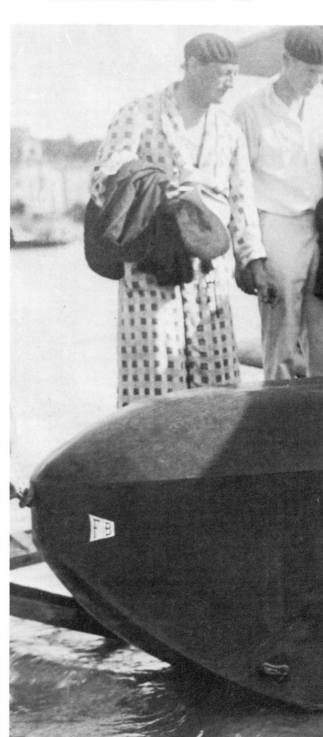

Left Mrs Ronnie Greville's butlers at Polesden Lacey. Unlike many other country house owners, Mrs Greville, heiress to a great Scottish brewing fortune and one of society's top hostesses, found little need to cut down on her staff.

Below Guests in some houses were not so lucky.

Above Lady Louis Mountbatten on the terrace at Port Lympne, flanked by Philip Sassoon and Lord Mountbatten.

———

Opposite Lord Louis ('Dickie') Mountbatten.

HOUSES

Above Chiswick House, Middlesex, designed by the 3rd
Earl of Burlington in 1725. The wings, designed by
James Wyatt, were added in 1788. When this
photograph was taken in the summer of 1861, the Duke
of Devonshire had lent the house to his sister, the
Dowager Countess of Granville. Amongst the guests
strolling on the lawns are (*left to right*) Lady Rivers (Lady
Granville's daughter), Lady Mary Alford, the Hon.
Fanny Pitt (Duchess of Leeds), the Hon. Blanche Pitt,
the Hon. Frederick Leveson, Lady Mary Wood
(Viscountess Halifax) and Emily Wood.

———

Opposite top Helmingham Hall, Suffolk, seat of the
Tollemache family.

Above Seaforde, county Down, seat of the Forde family.

Above Weston Park, Shropshire, designed by James Paine *c.* 1765, seat of the earls of Bradford. Photographed by the 2nd Earl's daughter, Lady Lucy Bridgeman.

Above Harlaxton Manor, Lincolnshire, designed by Anthony Salvin for the Gregory family.

———

Opposite, left to right (top) Lambton Castle, Durham, seat of the Earl of Durham, was designed by Ignatius Bonomi. Originally built at the end of the eighteenth century, it was later altered/Bedgebury Park, Kent, an early nineteenth-century house transformed by R. C. Carpenter into a French Renaissance château. Home of Alexander Beresford-Hope; (middle) Eaton Hall, Cheshire, seat of the Duke of Westminster, designed by Alfred Waterhouse/Clumber House, Nottinghamshire, seat of the dukes of Newcastle. Originally by Stephen Wright, it was extensively altered after a fire in 1879; (bottom) Highclere Castle, Hampshire, built for Lord Carnarvon by Sir Charles Barry/Wimpole, Cambridgeshire, seat of the earls of Hardwicke.

Top Waddesdon Manor, Buckinghamshire,
designed by G. H. Destailleur for Baron Ferdinand de
Rothschild.

Above Tring Park, Hertfordshire, another
Rothschild house. Baron Rothschild, who was famous
for his vast insect collection, also kept exotic animals in
his park.

Right Taplow Court, home of the Grenfell family,
near Maidenhead, Berkshire. The lady in the
photograph is Lady Cynthia Graham.

ACKNOWLEDGEMENTS

The preparation of *Country House Camera* has taken me all over Great Britain and Ireland, and into the homes of many different people. In all of these, I have been given the greatest assistance with my project, and for their trust, help and hospitality I am therefore equally indebted to the following: the Marquess and Marchioness of Anglesey, the Marquess of Bath, Sir Martyn Beckett, the Hon. Raymond Bonham-Carter, Richard Bridgeman, Mr and Mrs Hugh Cavendish, the Dowager Marchioness of Cholmondeley, Alec Cobbe, Lady Silvia Combe, Mr and Mrs Robin Compton, the Earl and Countess of Derby, the Duke and Duchess of Devonshire, Maureen, Marchioness of Dufferin and Ava, the Marquess and Marchioness of Dufferin and Ava, Alexander Dunluce, Lord and Lady Egremont, Lord Erne, the Countess of Feversham, the Earl and Countess Fitzwilliam, Patrick and Anthea Forde, Lord and Lady Gage, the Knight of Glin, Lord Grimthorpe, the Hon. Desmond Guinness, the Earl and Countess of Halifax, Major and Mrs Hamilton, Mark Haywood-Booth and the staff of the Prints and Photographs Department of the Victoria and Albert Museum, Miles Hildyard, the staff of the Irish National Trust Archive, Lord and Lady Lambton, the Earl of Leicester, the Hon. Patrick Lindsay, Julian and Victoria Lloyd, Professor Anthony Malcomson and the staff of the Public Record Office of Northern Ireland, the Hon. Mrs Martin, John Michell, the Earl and Countess of Pembroke, Sir Eric and Lady Penn, Sean Rafferty, the Earl of Shelburne, Lord and Lady Christopher Thynne, Lord Tollemache, Mr and Mrs Reggie Winn, and Christopher Wood.

In addition, I must also mention that I have unashamedly drawn on the wealth of information collected by Mr Mark Girouard in his superb book, *Life in the English Country House*.

Once again, I must pay tribute to the helpfulness and skill of photographers Bob Ireland and Geoff Goode, the hard work and beautiful design of Max Fairbrother, and the excellent editing of Brigid Avison.

Finally, this book would not be what it is, had it not been for the constant and valuable assistance and ideas of Mark Boxer. Thank you all.

Lord Boothby's description of Trent Park which appears on page 187 is taken from his book, *I Fight to Live*, published in 1947 by Victor Gollancz Limited.